# Retirement Sparks
## Reigniting the Passion for Life–
## Irreverent Observations
## on Retirement

*Hope you enjoy this.*

*Elaine Decker*

# Other published work from Elaine M. Decker

*New York Times*

New Jersey Opinion: Sep 18, 1988
"Please Send One Bag of Garbage"
http://www.nytimes.com/1988/09/18/nyregion/new-jersey-opinion-
please-send-one-bag-of-garbage.html

New Jersey Opinion: July 17, 1988
"Commuter Calls It Quits"
http://www.nytimes.com/1988/07/17/nyregion/new-jersey-opinion-
commuter-calls-it-quits.html

*Marketing News:*

Viewpoint: May 11, 1992
"Being green is not as easy as it seems"

Viewpoint: April 15, 1991
"An open letter to Jim Manzi, Lotus president"

*Privacy Journal*

December 2000
"How to Track Missing Cats and Stray Husbands"

July 1990
"Assault with Intent to Sell"

*Advertising Age*

December 4, 2006
Viewpoint: "No more ugly Betty"

# Retirement Sparks
## Reigniting the Passion for Life–
## Irreverent Observations
## on Retirement

by Elaine M. Decker

Published by Business Theatre Unlimited

ISBN-13: 978-1468095708
ISBN-10: 1468095706

*To Jagdish,*
*who gave me a reason*
*to look forward to retirement and*
*who helps keep the spark alive.*

*and*

*To Sheryl,*
*whose untimely passing*
*made me realize*
*we should start following*
*our passion today.*

iv

# Contents

# Contents (cont.)

Page

# Contents (cont.)

## Page

# Contents (cont.)

Page

# Contents (cont.)

## Page

# Introduction

I've been writing social satire for over twenty-five years. Until now, much of what I've written was shared only with friends and co-workers. Selected pieces were carried by publications that reach a national audience, encouraging me to keep writing. My opinion columns have appeared in the Sunday *New York Times* (now available on-line,) *Marketing News* and *Privacy Journal*. I've also had several letters to the editor published in *Time* magazine and *Advertising Age*.

*RetirementSparks* came about when I began laying the groundwork for my retirement. The process to apply for Medicare was confusing and the paperwork I received from providers pitching products was pervasive. I decided to start blogging about it at *RetirementSparks.blogspot.com*.

Over time, my topics broadened from Medicare and Social Security to downsizing, planning and other retirement-related issues. I write about the adjustments people make as they move into retirement life. Selections from my weekly blog now appear in the monthly RI publication, *Prime Time*. As with my printed pieces, my blog humor is edgy, irreverent and self-deprecating.

This book includes what I consider to be the best posts from the first year or so of *RetirementSparks*. It also includes two earlier pieces that I feel will be of interest to those approaching retirement.

The first of these originally appeared as the *Philosophy Corner* of my 2006 holiday newsletter. *Quality of Life—It's as Easy as A, B, C* offers a way to think about the years leading up to retirement. It ends this Introduction.

The second piece will likely appear in a future *RetirementSparks* post. *Just One Tasteful Tattoo* provides a fitting end, both literally and figuratively. It appears in the *Epilogue.*

About half of this book was written while I was still employed. I'm now retired and able to devote more time to my writing. I'll continue to blog about how to reignite that spark for life. You can sign up through blogspot to have RetirementSparks.blogspot.com posts emailed to you.

## Quality of Life—It's as Easy as A, B, C

Originally Published Dec. 2006

This *Philosophy Corner* comes from an "aha" moment I had a few months ago. I was crunching some numbers to figure out how our lifestyle might need to change if we stay in the Oriole house until I "retire" at age 66.

Let's begin with working definitions of various qualities of life. An "A" quality life is one where you never think about money. Cost is never an issue. You buy and spend whatever you want.

A "B" life is one where you don't really want for anything. You give some thought to your expenditures, but only in rare circumstances will you deny yourself something you really want because of the cost. This presumes, dear reader, that you are someone with modest tastes. Or can at least try to be.

A "C" quality of life means you think very carefully before you purchase anything not in your budget. You still have some discretionary money, but you spend it very carefully.

Here's a real world example. If I led an "A" life, I'd have my tree trim catered and use real china (rented.) In a "B" life, I'd use disposable cups and plates and utensils and toss them after the party. In a "C" life, I'd use disposables, but I'd wash the plastic ones after the party and use them again. By the way, in a "D" life, you can't afford parties.

Back to my retirement plan. Ever my father's daughter—he was painfully conservative, I put together a plan that assumes I will not earn a penny in retirement. I'll live off my three-legged stool (of pension, social security and IRA draw of 3-4%). It allows for expenses that net to a guarantee of a "B" quality of life, barring anything extraordinary.

Back to today. My latest job (in non-profit) served up a 25% pay cut vs. my prior positions. So, I was planning to live a "C" life now, in order to protect a "B" future. As my "aha" moment dawned, I realized that I'm living a guaranteed "C" for a future "B." But that "B" could very well turn out to be an "A" if I earn anything at all after I retire.

Even with just the three conservative legs, my retirement life would at worst be a "C." It seems reasonable to expect that my writing could generate some modest income. My stool could have a fourth leg, though perhaps a stubby one.

That's when I decided: *Why not live my "B" life now?* I may yet get the "B" life later, but even if not, it will net out the same (one phase a "B;" one phase a "C"), Which means, I'm really enjoying myself now and I'm not worrying if I dip into my retirement egg a bit. *Don't worry, Dad. I'll be careful to not invade the principal.*

Quality of life really is as easy as "A, B, C." I went for the "B" and threw out the plastic stuff after the party that year. It felt liberating! Some friends with whom I've shared this concept have decided to go for an "A" life now, and I say *bravo!* to them.

Here's my advice: Whether it's "A," "B" or "C,"

*Live your best letter now!*

# Section I

# Social Security,
# Medicare
# and Other Healthcare Issues

# Putting A Toe Into the Water of Retirement

Original Post Date Sep. 1, 2010

Today marks Day 1 of being on Medicare.

My new mantra:

*If Medicare is here, can Social Security be far behind?*

It certainly wasn't easy getting here, despite some guidance and suggestions from friends who are a few months or years ahead of me on this.

Now I ask you, why, when Medicare has Part A, Part B, and Part D, would our otherwise nurturing government title its options for your selection Plan A, Plan B, etc.?

I don't know about you, but when I'm drowning in paperwork—at least three copies of everything were sent by AARP alone, the last thing I need is to have two sets of four-letter words that both begin with P and have the letters A and B, all floating around in the material I'm supposed to be evaluating. Especially when the AARP packages have pages that got separated so you couldn't tell what all the different entries meant. Future mailings came with them stapled, by the way.

So for days I was trying to make sense of Plan A thinking I was reading something about Part A. And of course, no sense was to be made, no matter how many times I read it. I don't like feeling stupid, no matter how much wine I've had to drink. I especially don't like being forced to wonder if I'm already having Senior Moments and I'm not even retired yet.

My "Aha Moment" (thank you, Oprah) came when I received the stapled version and discovered that row one under the heading Plan A was actually Part A and row two was Part B, etc. *"Aha!"* (said I). *"This is really just an Excel spreadsheet that was missing its Column A labels!"* It still took awhile to figure out what made the most sense for me (calculating expected out of pocket based on current number of doctor's visits, etc.) But at least I was finally playing with a full deck. And a fresh bottle of wine.

So, in service to those of you who are still looking forward to Medicare, I offer the following:

NOTE TO GOVERNMENT: Please consider renaming Plan A and Plan B etc.:
Plan 1 and Plan 2 etc.
Or better yet, how about:
Cheapest Plan, Next Cheapest Plan, Travel Lovers Plan, and You've Got To Be Kidding Me Plan.

Just can't wait to see what comes next...

# The Complexities of Simplification
Original Post Date Sep. 7, 2010

One of the most common goals of retirement is to simplify life. The day that my Medicare began, I went from one health insurance card to three—basic Medicare, supplemental coverage and prescription coverage. I wasn't on it for even a week when a fourth card arrived in the mail. What part of "simplify" does the government not understand?

The fourth card is for prescriptions that aren't covered by the third card, but it costs nothing. The papers that came with it say I should be sure to use the third card before using the fourth one. Of course, they don't refer to them as cards three and four. They are the card for Part D and the card for "the AARP Prescription Discount Program." If the discount program card costs nothing and I received it without even asking, why isn't it just folded into Part D, the third card —which I also have through AARP? That would be too simple.

So let's get back to counting retirement cards. Four for my healthcare coverage, plus my AARP card, and I'm sure I'll get some type of card when I start collecting Social Security. That makes six and leaves me just one short of having a card for every day of the week. Which brings back fond memories of that set of embroidered panties I had in the sixth grade. The Saturday ones were my favorites. Sigh.

That in turn reminds me how my mother always told us to wear clean underpants each day. *"You never know when you might get hit by a truck and be rushed to the hospital. Think how embarrassing it would be if you had on dirty undies, or worse yet (gasp!) ones with holes."* I can see a lot of you smiling, because your mothers said the same thing to you.

But I bet when you were in kindergarten (and took the second bus), she didn't make you bring a brown paper bag with clean underpants for your brother in first grade (first bus). This because she couldn't find yesterday's pair, and it never occurred to her that he might have put them into the hamper. Talk about embarrassing. I'm not sure he's forgiven me to this day. I actually made him put them on, even when he insisted his were clean. My mother had made me promise to.

Since I seem to have your attention on this tangent, please raise your hands. How many of you turned this around on your mother your freshman year in college? When I came home with leopard print bikinis in my laundry, my mother was horrified. *"What if someone saw these?"* she wailed. Duh. Yes indeed, what if. One could always hope... To which I replied in my most innocent voice, *"Yes, but mother, if I got hit by a truck, at least I'd have on clean ones with no holes."* She was not amused.

And to think this all started with me counting healthcare cards. Mom always had a knack for making everyone smile. I guess she still does. Double sigh.

# Donut Holes and Paper Trails

Original Post Date Oct. 23, 2010

Yesterday I had my semi-annual checkup. It was the first time I used my new insurance—other than for prescriptions. I presented my Medicare card, but could not find the one for my supplemental coverage. I rooted through a rubber-banded stack of cards an inch thick. Bank card, AAA, two AARP, countless membership and contact cards, a variety of appointment paperwork as far ahead as next summer. But no United Health card.

I stood there feeling half-naked, as though I had been caught without my "Friday" panties. (See posting from September 7 for explanation on that.) By dumb luck, I had next month's bill in my purse, so they took my information from that.

Last night I scoured my purse for the missing card. It was there all along. That second AARP card I mentioned? A supplemental coverage card branded with their logo. The provider's name, United Health, was buried in the mice type.

This experience added fuel to a fire sparked by insurance paperwork that came last week. Since I have now completed my first month on Medicare, I received a report of my prescription drug claims for September. As I read it, I realized I was holding the first accounting of my march toward the infamous donut hole.

You've probably heard of the donut hole. It's that gap in coverage in a range of prescription drug payments. Coverage stops from $2,830 to $4,550 and then picks up again. I'm on several prescription medications, but if I'm ever taking so many drugs that I pass $2,800 a year in claims, I've been scarfing far too many donuts. Still, attention must be paid.

The report I received caused a bulb to light up. Not only do I now have multiple health insurance cards, I'll have to set up a complicated system to track my medical expenses. I'll need to record date of service, doctor's name, amount billed, date and amount paid by Medicare, ditto for supplemental coverage and for payments I make. I haven't met my deductible, so I'll need to track that, too.

I'm suddenly reminded of the later years of my mother's life. My sister would come from Vermont and spend a week with our mother in New Jersey every summer. One of Barb's tasks was to sort through all of Mom's medical expenses and payments so she could file any errant claims. There were few personal computers back then. Everything was posted to green ledger paper using a system our father set up years earlier.

Since I lived closer, I took our mother to doctors' appointments, on special shopping trips and out to dinner occasionally. The medical paperwork was Barb's contribution to Mom's care. I remember thinking even then that I had the better end of the deal. Now I feel I owe my sister big time.

Back to my present day paperwork. I was finally feeling somewhat in control again when a hefty packet arrived in the mail. Turns out we're about to enter the much-hyped "open enrollment period," that once-a-year window when we can change our health care coverage without penalty.

Be still my heart. I spent much of August figuring out what coverage I wanted. Do they really think that just two months later I'm going to change my mind? No comments, please. I suppose I should at least open the envelope and skim the contents. What if there's something I need to do even if I don't want to change plans?

My lack of knowledge embarrasses me. With my self-confidence waning, I'm compelled to check my panties to make sure I'm wearing the right day. I discover they're inside out, so I can't tell. At least they're clean and free of holes. My mother would be proud.

# Privacy vs. Accessibility

Original Post Date Nov. 3, 2010

My primary care physician is a partner in a large group practice. I trust him. If I didn't, I'd change doctors. At my recent check-up, I was handed a pamphlet and asked to sign up for an electronic health information network.

Given the litany of health issues I've had over the years, I appreciate the benefits of having all my medical information accessible to all the health care providers who might ever need to treat me. But what I read in the fine print in the pamphlet made my hair stand on end. Mice type always makes me skeptical. Seeing more than two paragraphs of it sets off alarm bells. This pamphlet has seven.

My health care life has become complicated enough since Medicare came along. It seems like going electronic could complicate it even more. The mice type starts out innocently enough; paragraph two lays out my HIPAA rights. *"I understand that health information is protected under federal privacy laws."* Good news. They recognize my right to privacy.

Not exactly. *"Providers... that access health information about me... may re-disclose this information to health care providers/organizations... for reasons unrelated to the coordination of my health care and treatment."* Wait a minute. Why would I want my private health laundry aired out for any reasons other than medical ones? Seriously. You might as well say you'll sell my name for marketing and fund raising purposes. I get enough junk mail already. I don't need to feed the beast.

If you're thinking: "That just comes with the territory," keep reading. It gets even better. *"This health information may be re-disclosed to a person or entity that is not... covered by federal privacy regulations, and therefore, is no longer protected by those regulations."*

So let me see if I have this straight. Privacy laws protect health information. However, in order to get better treatment, I need to be OK with giving my health info out to someone who has nothing to do with my treatment. And who, by the way, won't have to respect my privacy. I'm not surprised to see that behavioral health is one of the areas that might get re-disclosed. I'd have to be certifiable to want to sign up for this.

Wait! Another area that could get disclosed is alcohol abuse. I'll cop to more than a few glasses of wine a day, if they'll tell the local purveyor of spirits that I'm a wino. That should get me an email when Fat Cat Chardonnay is on super sale.

If I work this right, it could actually turn out to my advantage. My mother saw a podiatrist in her later life. I'll start that now if I can get an occasional free foot massage for those little piggies that go numb when I wear pointy shoes with high heels. That was never a problem when I was in my prime. I'll even spring for a dermatologist, if it nets me a jar of high-end fade cream for my age spots. My hands are starting to look like my mother's and that's scary.

Hmmm. They also share information on genetic diseases. I'm not sure what all that covers. I know that hypertension runs in my family. I've always wanted to try yoga for that. Maybe someone will offer me a discount on classes. Not the yoga with the weird breathing. And not the one that requires even remotely good balance. Just the plain vanilla type where you chant *"Om-m-m. Om-m-m. Om-m-m."* I think that's Hindi for *"I could really go for a glass of Fat Cat right now."*

Where do I sign?

# FDA To Issue Medicare Warnings

Original Post Date Nov. 17, 2010

You may have heard that the FDA recently unveiled proposed graphic warning labels for cigarette packs. The messages state that cigarettes cause strokes and heart disease, are addictive and cause fatal lung disease. The last message accompanies a photo of a dead body with a toe tag. Another comes with a photo of a corpse in a coffin.

I've just learned that the FDA is about to release another group of graphic warning labels—to accompany the Medicare insurance packets that we receive as we approach age 65. If you're squeamish, you may want to skip this post.

The first label reads: *"Warning! Filling out Medicare paperwork may cause you to have a nervous breakdown, requiring you to be restrained."* A photo of a demented-looking man in an old-fashioned straight jacket accompanies the text. He appears to be in a padded room.

Another cautions: *"Sorting through Medicare mailings may leave you clawing the walls and furniture."* The photo shows a woman kneeling, with arched back, shredding the arm of an overstuffed sofa. She reminds me of my cat sharpening her claws on the scratching post.

*"Take precautions! Initial review of Medicare material has been known to cause the reader to break out in a cold sweat."* The man in the photo sits shivering in a Snuggie blanket. Papers are scattered all around him, but he appears incapable of moving from his cocoon.

*"Reviewing your Medicare paperwork may make your hair stand on end. If you are doing this in the winter, beware of static electricity shocks."* The man in the photo clearly did not beware; even the hair on his forearms is at attention. Is that smoke coming out of his ears?

Here's a good one: *"Do not be alarmed by the drool that escapes the sides of your mouth as you prepare your Medicare application. This is a common occurrence."* Maybe so, but the mad-cowlike expression in the companion photo gives me pause. In my extensive experience, no good ever comes from a situation that leaves you slobbering.

My favorite reads: *"Danger! Careful reading of Medicare documents may cause you to go berserk and strangle anyone within reach."* This photo is like a caricature of a woman in the throes of severe PMS. The unwitting victim is no doubt her spouse, who probably asked when dinner would be ready. If only he had read the warning label.

The last one hits close to home. *"Contraindications for Medicare paperwork: Can cause your blood pressure to rise,* requiring extra medication and extra paperwork, setting you on a vicious cycle from which you will never recover. Remember Charlie on the MTA?" This is the only photo in color. It's me, with cheeks so red I look like I've just downed a bottle of Chianti.

You have to hand it to the FDA. They really know how to do warning labels. Here's one for them. *"Warning! Creating paperwork that frustrates seniors can be dangerous. Be careful opening mail from strangers."* The photo shows me again. I'm packing up half empty sardine cans, fur balls and other nasty looking stuff that's going to be ripe by the time it's delivered. The mailing label reads: Medicare Administration Offices.

Score one for us retirees.

# Acronyms for the Jargon
Original Post Date Dec. 15, 2010

Political commentators sure use a lot of acronyms. I'm not talking about ones used for texting, like "OMG" and "LOL." Theirs are strange. As I watched one of the political shows this past Sunday, I came to attention when I heard "BOMFOGers." The speaker explained that BOMFOG stood for "Brotherhood of Man, Fatherhood of God." He was warning viewers to be wary of those who spout meaningless platitudes. I think the term is a little like the onomatopoeic "bloviator," but with a more political focus.

My first thought was that BOMFOGer sounded raucously close to another word with an M and an F that ends in "er." My next thought was that acronyms can play a useful role in simplifying communications, especially in areas that are rife with jargon. I immediately realized that I could provide a valuable service by cataloging some acronyms for retirement.

Let's start with Medicare. I heard some of you moan, "Let's not!" It's a tough job, but someone has to do it. You should look carefully at a MSIP (Medicare Supplement Insurance Plan) to cover costs that basic Medicare doesn't. Part A covers hospital services. Part B covers medical expenses such as PSIOPMSSS, and PST, DT and DME. So, you've got your

Physicians' Services, In & Out Patient Medical & Surgical Services & Supplies; and also Physical & Speech Therapy, Diagnostic Tests and Durable Medical Equipment. I hope you've been paying attention, because there will be a test.

If you decide to get coverage for the prescription drugs you take, you'll enroll in a PDP (Prescription Drug Plan.) Be careful not to confuse that with AARP's PDP (Prescription Discount Program). The latter PDP is free and at this writing is run through Walgreens. It can be used when your regular PDP doesn't cover the prescription you're filling.

So, if your PDP doesn't pay for your medical marijuana, for example, AARP's PDP might. If you're smart, you'll toke before you even try to figure this one out. Especially since the fine print reads *"The AARP PDP is not a licensed pharmacy and may be discontinued at any time."* By the way, as best I can tell, bongs are not covered as DME.

Your PDP (Prescription Drug Plan) is where that infamous "donut hole" comes into play. The good news is, if you're really decrepit and take lots of meds, you can throw yourself on the mercy of drug companies' PAPs (Patient Assistance Programs). When you reach the donut hole, your PAP kicks in. If the AARP PDP has gone toes up, you won't get smeared.

Moving on to Social Security. We all know that FRA (Full Retirement Age) is the age at which our government finds we're sufficiently senile to collect 100% of earned benefits. For my peers, that's 66. However, 100% of earned benefits is not, in fact, the maximum we can receive. That's right, we can get more than 100% if we're willing to hang on until full senility sets in. The government has decided that for all of us that happens at age 70.

This means FRA is really FRABNAFMAB (Full Retirement Age, But Not Age For Maximum Available Benefits). It sets up a new concept: OFRA (Over-Full Retirement Age). It also sends you to actuarial tables to decide if you'll live long enough to make it worth waiting for MABRA, or whether you should take the money and run at FRA.

Once you decide to start collecting your Social Security benefits, you'll have the option for DDA (Direct Deposit Advice). When you choose that, your monthly payment will automatically appear in your designated account. Unfortunately for some of us, there is also the DDISEA (Direct Deposit Into Someone Else's Account). You may discover you have DDISEA even though you didn't sign up for it, and it takes close to an act of Congress to undo it.

I hope you have enjoyed this informative, if brief, foray into the topic of retirement acronyms. There are so many more that I could share with you, but I don't want to risk your having an attack of AFRJO (Acronyms for Retirement Jargon Overload). I'm quite sure that isn't covered under OPMS, although it just might qualify you to find relief in medical marijuana. They say that every cloud has a silver lining.

# Saving Social Security
Original Post Date Dec. 29, 2010

Those of us on the verge of retirement pay close attention to discussions of whether Social Security will go toes up in the near future. I believe I've stumbled upon a funding solution that will preserve Social Security for posterity.

My idea was inspired in part by arguments over the extension of the Bush tax cuts. A key issue was whether the cuts should be allowed to expire for the very wealthy. There were differing opinions of what income marked the transition to that status. Some numbers thrown about were $250,000, $500,000 and $1 million per year. As a side note: these discussions make me worry that I'm hovering dangerously close to poverty level.

The real key to my plan to save Social Security was modeled after the infamous donut hole of Medicare's prescription coverage. We need to create a Social Security donut hole, but not on the receiving end of the equation—on the payment side.

With the current system, workers stop paying in when their income reaches $106,800. My plan will give rich folks a break for a donut hole of income running from $106,800 to, say, $1 million. (It's not that I'm generous. I just don't have the patience to argue about the threshold to super-wealthy.) Earners once again begin paying Social Security taxes on income over $1 million. The political parties can fight over what percentage they should pay. Even if it's less than the percentage paid by the lower income folks, on those ethereal salaries, Social Security will be fully funded for the next millennium. Now don't you all feel better?

While I'm on the subject of political parties fighting over things that could impact Social Security, let's not forget the tax deal that Obama cut during the lame duck session of Congress. Democrats thought he caved too easily; Republicans thought they were tricked into supporting a stimulus package. Many pundits say they are both correct.

The December 12, 2010 edition of *Inside Washington* addressed this issue, and panelist Mark Shields caught my attention when he made this interesting observation. *"The question about every conservative who comes to office is does he have compassion, does he have a heart. The question about every liberal leader is does he have a backbone?"*

As I listened to this, the characters from The Wizard of Oz suddenly appeared before me. There was the Tin Man, lamenting his lack of a heart. Next to him, the Cowardly Lion wished for courage, which certainly sounded like a plea for backbone. It occurred to me that if Shields' observation is correct, we need new symbols for our national political parties.

We should replace the elephant with the Tin Man and the donkey with the Cowardly Lion. This makes a lot of sense in the current climate. After all, our political conversations seem to have moved on down the road to Oz, and we can't really be sure what we'll find behind that curtain.

I wonder if I got rid of my ruby slippers when I was thinning out my closet...

# Speedy Methuselah

Original Post Date Mar. 2, 2011

As my retirement draws closer, I'm wondering if my body is going to hold out until I finally stop working. It seems like each week, something else starts to ache, or stops functioning efficiently, if at all. For instance, my eye doctor suspects I'm developing glaucoma, which my mother had, putting me at risk. He has me seeing a specialist next week.

In the midst of my physical deterioration, however, I read something in *Time* magazine that gave me cause for celebration. The caption of the very short blurb read *"The Speedy Live Longer."*

As you can imagine, this caught my attention. I adjusted my 3.25 magnifiers to be sure I could read the small print. (Note to self: after retirement, see if *Time* has a large print edition that I can subscribe to.) The item reported on a study of adults over 65. In other words, the sweet spot of RetirementSparks readership.

Participants who walked faster—and I quote here: *"were 90% likelier to live at least 10 more years than those who walked at a pokier pace."* The theory is that how fast you walk indicates how well various body parts are functioning (heart, lungs, joints and muscles, to be specific.) The better those work, the longer you live.

This was wonderful news for me, because I've always been a fast walker. Though I don't walk as much now as I should, I plan to walk more once I stop working. And though I certainly walk a bit more slowly now than I did five years ago, it's still a relatively fast pace.

There are three very specific reasons why I'm so speedy. The first is that I'm short. I've always been short, and like many of you (I suspect), I'm getting a little shorter each year. In order to keep up with my walking partners over the years (and there've been quite a few), I had to take more steps to cover the same ground. That means I've always had to walk faster than they did.

The second reason is that I'm chronically late. That means that I'm always rushing to get wherever I'm going. This of course means that the portion of the trip that's on foot requires an extremely brisk walk, and sometimes even a run. I'm so used to walking at this pace, that it rarely occurs to me that I might be able to walk more slowly on occasion.

The third has a lot to do with the fact that I worked in Manhattan for 20 years, for most of which I commuted in from New Jersey. That involved walking from the Port Authority bus terminal to Park and 50th (opposite the

Waldorf) and back almost every day. Put that together with my chronic tardiness, and you can quickly figure out that I spent a lot of time jogging across town to catch my bus—or make it to a morning meeting.

Walking fast on that route was essential for reasons beyond saving time. I passed through some dicey areas along the way—areas where people had been mugged on more than one occasion. I had decided that if I walked briskly and with purpose, muggers would think: *"Not a tourist. Probably will fight back. Not worth the trouble. I'm gonna look for an easier mark; plenty of them to be found."* You'd never see me gawking at store windows or staring up at the tops of the buildings, no matter how interesting the architecture.

As a side note, my co-workers used to tell me that the normal expression on my face was halfway between neutral and negative. I imagine that the impression I gave would-be muggers was that I was a woman on a mission, not someone to be trifled with.

Little did I know that my vertically challenged stature, my bad habits and my less-than-sociable demeanor would wind up adding ten years to my life. I need to be sure I don't lose ground once I retire. That means finding walking partners who can keep up with me, preferably ones that don't expect me to smile.

Don't all rush to sign up at once…

# Retirochondria

Original Post Date Mar. 26, 2011

So many people are self-diagnosing by Googling their health symptoms that medical professionals have coined a new term: "cyberchondriacs." It describes those who get so immersed in health-related research online that they're sure they have dozens of ailments.

In my week of retirement I'm already more in tune with my body's aches and pains than when I was going to an office. Either our house is an environmental hazard, or the leisure time that retirement affords leads to physical introspection along with psychological.

Of course, there is a third possibility. Like many new retirees, I'm watching more TV. This will wear thin pretty quickly, but for now, I'm doing it just because I can. It seems every third commercial is for a remedy for some health issue. During a few of these commercials, I've noted that I have at least one of the symptoms described.

I'm then compelled to go online to learn more about whether my symptoms (morning stiffness and fatigue, for example) mean I have fibromyalgia (for example) or some other ailment for which treatment is less pricey. This leads to more research, and a sizable list of conditions that cause stiffness, fatigue and memory problems. I forgot to mention that one.

Although many of these are normal signs of aging, I'm drawn to the more exotic explanations. Simply put, I'm at risk of becoming a "retirochondriac." I'm sure there are thousands like me out there, perhaps too ashamed to admit it. Know that you are not alone. Step into the light.

Some of the information I've uncovered is alarming. I've been experiencing seemingly contradictory symptoms in my toes—both numb and at the same time tingly with sharp pain. A friend said it sounds like neuropathy, but I'm not so sure. When I checked these symptoms online, I discovered I might have been stung by a cone snail.

This is not that far fetched. From the photos, I recognized these critters as being among the shells displayed artistically in a china bowl in our living room. Some of you would say they are simply piled in the bowl, but you would be lacking creative vision.

Now I imagine the snails crawling around at night, looking for toes to sting. Laugh if you must, but I'm taking this very seriously. Severe cases of cone snail stings can lead to blurred vision (hm-m-m…) and respiratory paralysis. Note to self: ask eye doctor what he knows about cone snails.

Closer to home is the possibility that I have atrial fibrillation, which my mother had and which more than doubles one's likelihood of developing dementia after surviving a stroke. My mind is already wandering dangerously close to the outskirts of sanity. I don't need to add to my risk of dementia. The commercial for MULTAQ prompted me to learn the symptoms of AFib and where better to look than online?

Lack of energy—check, especially after a big meal (or a few glasses of wine…) Heart palpitations—check, but only when I lie awake at night thinking about everything I didn't get done. Dizziness—check, especially when I stand up suddenly (after a few glasses of wine). This is definitely something for my GP to investigate on my next visit.

While I was on WebMD, I researched one of my husband's symptoms. He's developed a quirk in his sleep—his legs twitch. Repeatedly. And at regular intervals. I assumed he has restless leg syndrome. Turns out it's Periodic Limb Movement Disorder, which happens only at night. Causes can include iron deficiency and anemia. He's been tired lately and needs more sleep. It's no wonder. You'd be exhausted, too, if you exercised all night.

His recent blood tests showed that his hemoglobin is low. His doctors have scheduled him for tests at a sleep clinic because they suspect he suffers from apnea, along with anemia. This diagnosis brought to you by the letter "A." If they just spent a little more time on WebMD—or in bed with him, they'd look into PLMD.

Time for one last symptoms search on WebMD. Let's see what we find for being exhausted (especially after clearing out a wall full of books). craving ice cream sandwiches (and a glass of Cab,) frequent trips to the loo (after lots of Cab), and mood swings (when I've run out of ice cream and wine). Well, what do you know! It looks like I may be pregnant. I guess I should cut out the wine, but who are we kidding. I'm as likely to do that as I am to be pregnant.

So much for self-diagnosis. Seriously, we need to be our own best health advocates. The more we understand our bodies and our baseline conditions, the better we can help our physicians keep us healthy. So, get on the Internet, research your symptoms and make your own list of ailments to annoy your doctor about. And don't forget to ask about cone snails.

# Social Insecurity
Original Post Date Apr. 13, 2011

In early April, 2011, I was worried that a government shut-down might delay the approval of my application for Social Security. I was skeptical that it would have been finalized in just one week; the process seemed suspiciously easy. Unfortunately, my suspicions were well-founded.

Over the weekend, I went on line to check the progress of my application. The status information indicated they'd sent me a request for proof of name change. I never received the request, but my guess is that they were referring to when I went back to my maiden name about 25 years ago.

Because I had a career as Dohn, I kept that name after my divorce. I changed back to Decker by court order in the mid-eighties. My Social Security earnings reports have been coming to Decker for as long as I can remember. My Medicare was approved for Decker. They can't seriously think I might still be Dohn. Oh, but they do. My disbelief turns to indignation that women have these problems, but men never do.

I spent Sunday sifting through paperwork looking for the court order to no avail. So, Monday morning I began what became hours of phone calls, surfing, and digging through filing cabinets. First I called the toll-free number from my on-line status information. Kenny answered. He was polite, but couldn't help me, since he was at the national level. Kenny redirected me to my local office in Providence.

Mrs. Dunlop also listened politely, but said there was nothing she could do. My application is being handled by Miss Katshow; she's the one who decided I need to prove I'm Decker. I'll need to convince her to remove the requirement. Mrs. Dunlop helpfully transferred me to Miss Katshow's extension, which was—not surprisingly—answered by her voice mail. I left a brief message.

My next series of calls were to the court in Elizabeth, New Jersey, (where the name change was done) to find out how to get a copy of the court order. Jim answered with good energy and encouraging enthusiasm. For a fleeting moment, I thought I might actually make some progress. Then Jim transferred me to Alan in the County Clerk's office.

Alan, who was not brimming with enthusiasm, impatiently explained that since this wasn't about deeds and mortgages, I needed another office. He sent me on to Arlene in Civil Assignment. She transferred me to Isabelle, who, Arlene assured me, was the person who could help. I practiced my positive thinking mantra while on hold. *Om-m-m. Om-m-m.*

Isabelle provided an address in Trenton where I could send a $25 check for a certified copy of the judgment to change my name. However, since I didn't know the exact year this happened and since it was at least 25 years ago, she also gave me a phone number for follow up. It was clear that Isabelle knew she was sending me on a fool's errand.

My next step was to Google the attorney who handled the name change. The bad news was he's now retired. The good news was that his phone number was listed through some network he's joined. The bad news was that led to yet another answering machine, so I left yet another message.

By now it was Monday afternoon. I made one more pass through some of our 20 plus file drawers. Perhaps I could find tax returns from the years before and after I went back to Decker. That would narrow the time of the court order, making my mail request more likely to be successful.

You'll be pleased to learn there is a God, because in the back of some of my old tax returns, I found the court order allowing me to become Elaine Decker again. I made a copy of the order and sent it certified to Miss Katshow.

At this writing, the status of my application still showed waiting for my proof of name change. I'll likely have to visit the Social Security office to resolve this. I'm retired now, so I have time for such projects. The Social Security administration probably counts on this. I wonder if Miss Katshow likes chocolate…

# AARP Bulletin Health Items

Original Post Date May 7, 2011

This month's *AARP Bulletin* came in today's mail. The feature item on hearing caught my eye: *"10 Things To Know About Improving It."* I've considered getting my hearing checked, so I decided to educate myself about the process.

It's not that I'm concerned about my ability to hear others, but I get the sense that I may be speaking louder than necessary. I base this on the looks I sometimes get from those around me. Well, the looks and the fact that people who are all the way across the room often chime in on my conversations.

The article noted hearing loss is linked to other health issues, in particular dementia and Alzheimer's, according to a recent study by Johns Hopkins and the National Institute on Aging. The risk of dementia is five times more for those with severe hearing loss, and double for those with mild loss. This makes sense. If you don't hear much of what's going on around you, the voices you're listening to are probably in your head.

The summary of the six types of hearing aids seemed especially helpful. It provided a brief description of each one, the pros and cons of each, and the costs. I read about all six, and I have some bad news: there is no perfect type of hearing aid. With each one, you'll have to give up something.

I hope James Dyson takes this on now that he has revolution-ized the vacuum cleaner and the hand dryers in public loos. He'll probably invent a hearing aid that also sucks out your ear wax and irrigates your sinuses.

Now for the really bad news. According to the article, Medicare doesn't pay for hearing aids, and also not for most hearing tests. I find this shocking. Medicare pays for eye exams. Who decided that seeing is more essential to healthy living than hearing? Is it worse to walk into a lamppost you didn't see? Or to be hit by a speeding car you didn't hear com-ing? And let's not forget the increased risk of dementia.

One of my college classmates has had compromised hearing and sight for much of her adult life. I remember her saying once that if she had to choose between going completely blind or completely deaf, she'd keep her hearing. That surprised me, so I asked why. She said she felt hearing was more essen-tial to social interaction. She was coming from a place of experience, so her words stayed with me.

Determined not to let the *AARP Bulletin* ruin my weekend, I leafed through the rest of the pages looking for some bright spot. It turned out to be an advertisement with vivid yellow background, a huge clump of Blackeyed Susans, and a couple in a gentle embrace. The woman was wearing a bright orange halter top and matching short orange sarong. You couldn't get much brighter than this ad.

The headline read: *"Sex. It's Never Too Late To Learn Something New."* The line is trademarked, by the way, so don't plan to use it as an icebreaker the next time you're at a cocktail party.

If the headline didn't get my attention, the subheads certainly did. *"See for Yourself on Discreet Home Video. Real people demonstrating real sexual techniques! Nothing is left to the imagination!"*

I hate to burst their marketing bubble, but I've reached the age where I'd rather leave real sexual techniques to the imagination. Their "visual encyclopedia" sounds like TMI for me.

As I tossed the bulletin into my recycling bin, I felt disappointed by the organization that is supposed to be looking out for me in my newly retired state. I expected more from AARP. They left me feeling distinctly un-cheery.

A vision flashed through my head. I'm locked in a tender embrace with my husband, and I'm whispering sexual fantasies. From the other side of the wall that separates our new condo from the neighbors comes a male voice. *"Hey, Buddy. It's never too late to learn something new."*

Then I had an even more disturbing thought. Those sex tapes are probably covered by Medicare.

# Sneaking Exercise

Original Post Date May 14, 2011

My first thought when the flier boldly titled *"Renew"* arrived in the mail was: *"AARP has redeemed itself."* The mailing came hot on the heels of the bulletin with the sex video ad and was subtitled: *"Easy Ways To Sneak Exercise into Your Day."*

On closer inspection, clarity and disappointment set in. The clarity was that the flier came not from AARP, but from my supplemental health care provider licensed to use their logo. The disappointment was that by the end of paragraph one, I was promised only a way to maintain my weight, not lose any. Since I'm now at my maximum weight ever, the last thing I want to do is maintain it. Searching for that glass half full—and hoping it will contain some red wine, I read on.

The first tip was: *"Bending and lifting keep your body in motion."* Unfortunately, my problem is not so much keeping my body in motion as it is getting it in motion in the first place. Furthermore, they recommended reaching higher as a way to increase calories burned. In my extensive experience, reaching higher is a reliable way for someone under 5 feet 2 inches to pull a muscle, thus making it even harder to overcome inertia for the next few days.

The flier also suggested hefting cans of beans a few times when unloading groceries, using them like hand weights. In our kitchen we use mostly fresh vegetables, but I assume canned soup would do. However, there are three sets of hand weights of varying poundage in the house. If I don't heft them, it's not likely I'll be inspired to heft soup cans, other than to stretch too high to put them into the cupboard. If we're talking wine bottles, that's a whole different story. If I pull my back out pumping wine, I can just open a bottle and drink away the pain.

There was also a little trick for when you're stuck in line at the bank—or the Social Security office. *"Boost your balance by standing on one foot, then the other."* I don't know about you, but if I saw someone shifting from foot to foot, I'd figure they were desperate for a bathroom. That's one of the problems that have not yet caught up with me in retirement. I have no desire to make folks think it has, but if it helped me move up in line, I might consider it.

The tips on sneaking exercise ended at the bottom of page one. Page two provided a safety check list. Halfway down it urged me to make sure that frequently used items are stored in cabinets within easy reach. I hate to be picky. Actually, that's not true. I love being picky. It's one of my more endearing traits. Just ask my husband.

Anyway, it seems to me that the *"put it where it's convenient"* advice flies in the face of *"find ways to reach even higher."*

Retirement Sparks

Are they deliberately trying to confuse me? Or is this a test to see if I'm paying attention? Maybe the "sneaky" in the headline wasn't about the exercise after all. Maybe it was about the editor. If so, here's a message for Sneakypants. *"Put it where it's not at all convenient."*

I should be more charitable. At least they didn't have mid-afternoon quickies as one of the ways to sneak some exercise into my day. The contradictions probably weren't intentional. Maybe they hired a cadre of retirees to write the articles and then some lazy, sloppy, not-yet-retired editor plopped them into the flier without taking time to read it as a unified piece.

If that's the case, I have some advice for Sloppypants about proofing for continuity and clarity. [For those who missed last week's post, it's from the headline in the AARP sex video ad.] *"It's never too late to learn something new!"*

Come to think of it, maybe pumping wine isn't such a bad way to sneak some exercise after all. I'll drink to that.

# No Longer Vicodin Virgin

Original Post Date Jul. 2, 2011

News flash! I'm no longer a Vicodin Virgin. I think everyone in my circle of friends and relations has taken that pain management medication at some point. Until yesterday, I had not.

My back and neck had been bothering me off and on lately. I attributed it to all the hefting and hauling of stuff from the upper floors to the basement in preparation for putting the house on the market. The house was finally listed on Thursday, and that's the day my body gave out. It's as if it knew all the work was done and it was finally okay to fall apart.

With the holiday weekend coming up, I didn't want to risk a visit to an ER if things didn't improve. I've spent enough holidays there with friends and family members. My own doctor was taking a long weekend, so I saw another doctor in his practice. She diagnosed severe muscle spasms, said she could actually see the swelling in my neck area on the right side. I left with prescriptions for hydrocodon and acetaminophen (generic of Vicodin) and cyclobenzaprine (generic of Flexeril).

Since I'd never taken either of these medications before, I decided to carefully read the paperwork that came with them.

By the time I finished, I concluded that I might as well spend the next few days in bed.

The medication for my muscle spasms advised me: *"If your condition does not improve in 2-3 weeks, contact your doctor."* I have news for them. If my condition doesn't improve in 2-3 days I will have killed myself or I'll be in jail for attempting to kill someone else.

I noticed that both meds list drowsiness and dizziness as side effects. What they really mean is you are so tired you sleep most of the day. And night. This is actually a good thing. My neck and back pain were so severe that I couldn't find a position that would enable me to sleep, so I can use a few days rest. As for the dizziness, have you ever been on the Tilt-A-Whirl at an amusement park? If you remember how you felt when you first stepped off that ride, you know how you feel on these meds. So much for driving.

Both meds indicate constipation among the possible side effects. I suppose if it's strong enough to stop the spasms in my back muscles it could pretty much shut down all the muscle activity in the body. But wouldn't that lead to diarrhea? I decided I don't really want to know.

Both also warn: *"Don't... do any activity that requires alertness until you are sure you can perform such activities safely."* There's not a heck of lot that I do that doesn't require alertness. Even this post, for example, requires me to coordinate my fingers on the keyboard so I hit the right letters. Which pretty much gets me back to sleeping. Or maybe watching TV.

Hydrocodon can cause nausea. Once again, I'm befuddled. My pain was so severe at one point that I actually thought I was going to throw up. I was looking forward to having the pain medication help me get rid of that symptom, not cause it.

Cyclobenzaprine notes dry mouth as a possible side effect. They should have warned that you'll get so thirsty you'd fight the dog to drink out of the toilet, if you had a dog.

My favorite part of this reading material is the long list of possible drug interactions. I'm disappointed, but not surprised, that I can't have wine while I'm taking this stuff. You can learn a lot by reading about the drugs that are contraindicated. I had no idea there was a class of drugs called "narcotic antagonists." What does that mean? Does morphine smack acetaminophen in the face and taunt: *"C'mon, sissy pants. Whatcha gonna do about it?"*

I know what I'm going to do about it. I'm going upstairs to take my evening dose of both meds and then I'm going to bed. Again. But first I'm going to put a large pitcher of water on the night table.

# Chia Fiber Alert

Original Post Date Jul. 6, 2011

Recent TV ads for chia seeds have caught my attention. Yes, these are the same chia seeds used in those ubiquitous Chia Pets that just won't go away. I call them counter top topiary for the masses. It seems those seeds have exceptional nutritional value, in addition to their decorative use.

First and foremost, according to the ads, they're an excellent source of fiber. At this point in our lives, who isn't interested in finding new sources of fiber? I'll try anything to keep me from dependence on those daily doses of Metamucil that were a staple of my mother's diet.

Some quick surfing of the Internet informed me that chia seeds were an important part of the ancient Mayan and Aztec diets. Those cultures prized chia seeds as a source of nutrition and energy. The chia plant *Salvia hispanica* grows throughout much of Central America and southern Mexico.

In addition to its benefit for fiber, chia is a great source of Omega 3 fatty acids, which promote circulation and cardiovascular health, and—according to some websites—help reduce inflammation due to arthritis and may even prevent Parkinsons. "How great a source of Omega 3?" (you may be asking). One ounce of chia seeds has more than two and a half times the Omega 3 as the same amount of flax seed (4.9 grams vs. 1.8.)

As for soluble fiber, an important aid in fighting high cholesterol, one ounce of chia seeds delivers 10.6 grams of fiber, while 3/4 cup of oatmeal gives you just 2.8, and one ounce of flax seeds provides 7.6. I read that chia seeds can absorb about ten times their weight in water and will turn to gelatin if left long enough. This has me wondering if Chia Pets look like they're wearing too much product as their "hair" grows.

As if omega 3 and good fiber weren't enough, we're told that chia seeds have three times the calcium as a stalk of broccoli and scads more protein than an equal amount of kidney beans. (No mention of how it compares with beans on musical side effects.)

They're also a rich source of potassium, magnesium, iron, and more. The full list sounds like the labels on all the vitamins we take every day in our household. Maybe I can just substitute chia seeds for my handful of pills and my daily banana. Those on gluten-free diets will be glad to know that chia seed flour can be used as a 1-to-1 substitute for wheat flour in any recipe.

Armed with all this impressive information, I purchased a supply of these magic seeds and added them to our diet.

We've had them sprinkled on our cereal and in our yoghurt and mixed into tofu burgers. It turns out there's a darker side to this wonder food that the ads don't share and the websites don't report.

Two weeks into my experiment, I noticed some hairy side effects. Suddenly, my navel was sprouting chia grass. Likewise, my husband's ears and underarms. We were becoming human Chia Pets. At first I tried trimming the sprouts, but the more I trimmed, the thicker it came in. Now we looked like human topiaries.

Fortunately, once we stopped ingesting the seeds, the growth died off. I share this sad tale with all of you so that you won't be suckered in by the ads, as I was. Alas, there is no magic bullet for getting enough soluble fiber and Omega 3 fatty acids. My advice: stick with your flax seed and oatmeal. And wash it all down with a nice glass of wine.

# Smile for Longevity

Original Post Date Jul. 13, 2011

I pride myself on being a "glass half full" kind of person. My husband has pushed this concept even further with his "overflowing glass" perspective. Numerous studies have shown that having a positive attitude boosts one's immune system. The results: less illness and faster recoveries.

The latest *Oprah* magazine has an article that provides yet another tool for a retiree's quest for longevity—smiling. That's right, the more you smile, the longer you'll live. What's more, the broader your smile, the longer your lifeline.

Unlike my other favored sources of posting ideas (the *New York Times* and *Time* magazine, to name just two), *Oprah* the magazine does not cite the source of the study being reported. But we all know that Oprah the person would not lie to us, so I'm sure this smile information is rock solid.

We are told that the method used was to look at photos of 230 baseball players in an old issue of *Baseball Register*. The players with "bigmouthed beams" outlived the glum ones by 7 years; they outlived the players with "partial smiles" by 4.9.

We're not given any guidance as to what qualifies as partial vs. bigmouthed. I'm guessing it has to do with either the number of pearly whites that are exposed, or perhaps the percentage of facial width that the smile takes up.

I'm actually less curious about that information than what possessed the person conducting the study to go to the *Baseball Register* in the first place. Are baseball players friendlier than football stars? They probably have more teeth than hockey players. But why use athletes in the first place?

Perhaps they started with photos of Miss America contestants and then realized that they all had "bigmouthed beams," hence providing no range of data to measure. And shame on those of you who were thinking "big headlights."

This brings me to another point in the *Oprah* article. It identified two types of smiles—genuine and fake. "Big whup!" I hear you saying; "we all knew that." I'll bet you didn't know you can weed out the phonies by looking at their eyes. A genuine smile causes—I'm quoting here—*"a facial muscle called the orbicularis oculi"* to contract, *"crinkling the skin around the eyes."*

Supposedly, you can't fake an o.c. contraction. Keep it clean now. When you see lines at the corners of the eyes, you know it's a genuine happy face. Frankly, I'm not so sure about this. I've seen a lot of people, women in particular, who've spent far too much time in the sun and are left with permanent crinkles around their eyes. But since this is about extending your own life, it doesn't matter whether other people are sincere.

This of course leads to the question: What can we do to help us smile more often and more broadly? And I suppose more genuinely, otherwise we might not get the health benefit. One simple way is to read RetirementSparks on a regular basis. Sorry. That's shameless self promotion and quite rude.

We do know that positive attitudes and good moods are contagious. *Oprah* cites the *British Medical Journal* as the source. Hang around with happy people and you're more likely to be happy, so pick your friends accordingly. Try this simple screening of potential friends: "Are you a glass half full or a glass half empty person?" Go with half full —or overflowing—every time.

Practice smiling in front of the mirror. *Oprah* says smiles are contagious. Even if you start with a fake one, when you see it in the mirror, pretend it's someone else and just smile back. What may have started as fake will become genuine. This is my own idea, not *Oprah's*, so if it works, give me the credit.

Other things in life usually bring smiles, like little children and animals. If you don't have these in your own household, visit a local playground or dog park. You can smile vicariously at the antics of the offspring and pets of others. Just be careful you don't look creepy doing it. Not everyone reads *Oprah*, so you could have a hard time explaining your motives.

Of course, there's always one of my favorite ways to bring a smile to my face. Open up a nice bottle of wine, sit back, relax, and just smile, smile, smile.

# Weep Not, Wine Lots

Original Post Date Aug. 8, 2011

Common wisdom says that crying is a good way to relieve stress and depression. Weep away all that bad karma and get it out of your system! Turns out, common wisdom may be wrong.

A recent study reported in the *Journal of Research in Personality* had about 100 women in the Netherlands keep diaries for several months noting their moods and crying habits. The authors found that in 61% of the crying jags, the women felt no better and no worse than before they spilled all those tears. Fewer than one third had improved moods and 9% actually felt worse after letting it all out. An interesting side tidbit was that most of the subjects cried when and where they thought no one else could see them.

If you feel like crying now that you know weeping may not perk you up, I know something that will. *Advertising Age* just reported some good news about the on-line wine business. Persistence and an accumulation of state legislative changes have sweetened the pot for on-line vino vendors. On July 1, Maryland became the 38th state to allow out-of-state wineries to ship their product into the state. This trend has enabled on-line vendors to attract capital and expand their businesses.

Wine.com posted its first ever profit this fiscal year; it sold 2 millions bottles in the past year. You've probably heard of flash mobs. Well, WineShopper is a flash-sale website set up by Wine.com. Its daily emails offer its users discounts of up to 70%. The catch? They're good for only 72 hours. It's kind of like Groupon on steroids. A recent special was 1 cent shipping on orders of $99 or more. Specials count down in the web page header, much like an EBay auction. Ends in 3 hrs 40 min!

Lot18 has snared $13 million in funding from VCs; it acts as a middleman between wineries and oenophiles. Its wine "curators" select the wines and send out daily email reviews. Their CEO boasts that their site is so popular and their selections so good that some of their choices never even make it to bricks and mortar purveyors.

I think these websites are God's gift to retirees who like to nestle into their favorite chair and relax with a really good glass of wine. In other words, gifts to me. Now we can even order our wine while we're nestled in, provided we have a wireless router. Note to self: get one of those when we move to Vermont.

So the next time you're feeling stressed or depressed, don't go off by yourself and get weepy. It probably won't make you feel better. Just go off by yourself and enjoy an excellent bottle of wine. Don't worry. There's no more shame in drinking alone than there is in crying alone in some hidden, dark corner.

If you're like most of us and have a life that's quite stressful, you'll plan ahead and have that wine waiting for you when you feel a crying jag coming on. While you're drinking the one you have in stock, be sure to go online to order a few replacement bottles. But you'd better hurry. That deal on shipping ends soon!

# Fat Is Good, Sometimes

Original Post Date Aug. 17, 2011

At last, some news that actually puts a spring in my retirement step. A recent study written up in York University's *Faculty of Health News* blog shows that, under certain conditions, people who are obese are actually less likely to die of cardiovascular causes than skinny folks.

The study was conducted by a team of mostly Canadian scientists over a 16-year period and was published in the journal *Applied Physiology, Nutrition and Metabolism*. The team compared the mortality risk of 6,000 obese Americans with that of lean subjects. Although not stated in the summary, one assumes the lean ones were also Americans, though I'm not sure that would have made a huge difference.

Here's the catch. The chubby folks had to already be a tad overweight as young adults and had to have been less obsessed with losing weight than the lean folks. That is, they would have tried less often throughout their lives to lose weight.

The pleasingly plump also had to have no serious *"physical, psychological or physiological impairments."* I did not dig deeply enough to get the details on what impairments made this list. In my experience, the Canadians have a much higher tolerance than Americans for non-conforming behavior, so I'd probably clear the hurdle on this one.

Apparently, being content with ones body, even if it was carrying a few more pounds than ideal, meant that these subjects were likely to have a healthy lifestyle. They were physically active and ate healthy food—though probably too much of it.

That combination of activity and a balanced diet with lots of fruits and vegetables seems to lead to healthier hearts than yo-yo dieting.

I've been on more than an occasional diet throughout my life, but I can't say that I fall into the yo-yo category. I was more of a "special occasion" dieter. You know, upcoming vacation to a Club Med, good friend's wedding, high school or college reunion. By the time I reached my forties it was more like "important job interview." You can imagine how rare those were as I got older.

Moving on to one of my favorite medical subtopics, acronyms—the researchers for this study used—and I quote—*"a new grading tool, the Edmonton Obesity Staging System (EOSS)."*

This new tool was developed at the University of Alberta and has been shown to be more accurate than the more widely known and enormously popular BMI (Body Mass Index) in targeting folks who need to lose weight.

For those not familiar with the BMI, here's a layman's description of how it works. You fill a bathtub to the brim with water and plop your body into it. If the water that over-flows takes more rolls of paper towels to mop it up than you got on sale at Costco last month, you're probably too fat. Likewise, if you float when you get into the tub, you should think about toning up.

BMI is also sometimes shortened to the catchy "pinch an inch" criteria, meaning that if you can pinch more than an inch of fat anywhere on your body, your B has too much M. Or as my internist would so tactfully put it, "There's too much of you." Personally, I think that the fat under one's neck should be excluded from the pinch test for those over 60. Also upper arms for women over 55.

The EOSS incorporates the BMI, waist-to-hip ratio and some clinical measures of obesity-related medical conditions—such as hypertension and diabetes. High blood pressure runs in my family, and it caught up with me years ago, so I'm not sure how I would fare with the new grading tool. I figure I can't do any worse than I would with the old one, even disallowing my neck wattle and arm flaps.

The EOSS classifies five stages of obesity. The blog report does not itemize these, but after considerable digging, I've uncovered all five. If you recognize yourself as number three or higher, you need to lose weight even on the new EOSS scale.

The five stages are (from least obese to most:)

1. I bet everyone pinched your cheeks when you were a baby.

2. Did you forget your Spanx, or is that a seriously out of control muffin top?

3. This little piggy went to market, but apparently this little piggy forgot to go home.

4. Jiggle, jiggle, wiggle, wiggle. Is there any part of you that doesn't shake when you walk?

And the highest level:

5. EOSS, BMI—YAHO
(Forget how we measured it—You Are Hopelessly Obese.)

# Section II

# Downsizing
# for
# Retirement

**BEFORE**

**AFTER**

# Facing the Music

Original Post Date Sep. 4, 2010

For many of us, retiring means downsizing. Moving from a big house, reducing its contents, thinning out closets. Retiring can mean having to give up things we've owned and loved forever. The attraction may be illogical, but the more it's based on sentiment, the harder the decision. For me, downsizing is one of the most difficult aspects of retirement planning. It hits me with a double whammy.

For many years, I was an obsessive collector. I always felt that one of something was lonely and needed a friend. Once I made the pair, I was sunk. Because whenever I came across another related item, I was compelled to bring it home to introduce it to the others. You can see how this got totally out of hand.

Though I've managed to curtail the incoming additions, I have a problem breaking up the families that already live with me. If you haven't picked up on this already, I have a more serious problem than simply amassing stuff. I anthropomorphize almost everything, no matter how inanimate the object. So my double whammy is that I'm not just breaking up families, I'm parting with my children.

If I'm evaluating two wrought iron floor lamps, trying to decide which stays and which goes, I imagine the one I plan to discard saying, *"Why me? Why not him? Why am I not as lovable? Look how interesting MY shade is! Just put a stronger bulb in me, for heaven's sake!"*

I've concluded that the only way to thin out my collections is to get rid of each one in its entirety. This comes with its own problems. Take my collection of figural cookie jars. Please! I know there won't be room for them in a smaller home.

But as I prepare to sell them, I find myself thinking: *"Raggedy Ann and Raggedy Andy must be priced as a pair. Can't split them up,"* (even though she's perfect and he has a chip on his hat). And then, *"The tortoise and the hare really belong together."* (Never mind that my brother brought me the turtle from his trip to Guatemala, and the rabbit was made by one of my father's co-workers in her ceramic class and isn't even a cookie jar. It just looks like one.) And then, *"Chances are, the pig in the farmer's overalls and the elephant in the sailor suit will appeal to the same buyer. But wait! That leaves the cat in the French schoolgirl uniform all by herself..."*

Maybe somewhere out there is someone as obsessive as I am who will take the entire collection, intact. Yeah, right. And maybe someday pigs will fly. But if so, please don't let him leave without his friend, the elephant.

# Thinning Out the Closet
Original Post Date Sep. 5, 2010

Today I'm wading deeper into the topic of downsizing for retirement. About six months ago, I decided to tackle a major challenge—thinning out my closet. Or more accurately—closets. We have a big house and my clothes are spread throughout five closets. Yeah, I know. I'm pathetic. Adorable and well dressed, but pathetic. But I'm also a Virgo, so at least my closets are well organized.

As with my various collections (see 9/4/10 posting), I've been quite controlled about adding to my wardrobe in recent years. Generally, if something new comes in, something old needs to go out. That's helped keep my wardrobe from expanding—unlike my waist—but it hasn't helped cut it down.

A digression for my fellow clothes horses: one of the ways I curtail my buying: I estimate the number of times I expect to wear the item. If a top is going to cost me more than $5 per wearing, a bottom more than $10, and so on, I buy the item only if I need it for something special. That way, I can generally be sure that I'll really—as my mother used to say—"get my money's worth out of it." Of course, "special" is a relative term, but that's fodder for a whole other posting. Back to thinning out what's already in those closets.

I needed a plan of attack, and my assistant, Amy, describes the one I devised as my clothes "auditioning" for retirement. Since I'm still employed, I "dress" every day. Each night, I try on clothes for the next day, focusing on items that I rarely wear—things from the gray zone of whether or not to keep them. If the outfit looks bad or feels uncomfortable, the offending item goes straight to the donation pile. If it looks and feels OK, I wear it to work the next day.

At the end of the day, I evaluate how I thought I looked, as well as how "connected" I feel to the clothes. If I feel good about the outfit, it's a keeper. If I don't, it goes into the laundry on its way to the donation pile.

Amy has become an enthusiastic participant in this process. When I'm wearing something she hasn't seen before, she asks, *"Is that auditioning?"* If she likes the outfit, she gives it encouragement, *"I hope you make the cut!"* When I tell her something just doesn't feel or look right, she waves to it and says wistfully, *"Goodbye, skirt!"*

I've thinned out a lot of clothes this way, but I'm still two closets over a retirement wardrobe. Any slacks—other than wool ones—that need dry cleaning get donated. Likewise blouses that need ironing. The dress that I affectionately but morbidly referred to as "my mother's funeral dress"—now far too small—gone.

I know I probably don't need 18 pairs of black pants, 30 black tops, and 20 pairs of black shoes—and yes, I counted them. But the pants are different cuts and weights, and the tops have different necklines and sleeve lengths. And the shoes, well, did I mention my co-workers used to call me Imelda Decker?

If any of you have suggestions on how to refine this audition process, please share them. I have nightmares that a month after I've donated one of my former favorites, I'm looking for it to wear to some "special" occasion. I just hope it's not a funeral.

# Condensing the Bookshelves
Original Post Date Oct. 6, 2010

Almost everyone who is downsizing for retirement has to face the daunting process of condensing shelves full of books. I've finally psyched myself up to attack this task. I begin with the bookshelves in the second floor hall, scanning groupings from top to bottom.

There's the Women's Lib section. Excuse me... Women's Empowerment. I think I can part with *The Female Eunuch* and not put my self esteem at risk. There was a time when I might have thought *Sexual Politics* was an oxymoron; now it sounds like redundancy. As I recall, *Men—An Owner's Manual* was not much help when I first got it. It doesn't seem like a title that would improve with age.

I need the step stool to see the titles on the top shelf. There's an entire section of poetry that I would have bet I had tossed two moves past. I count eight volumes of Rod McKuen. He was too cool in the sixties. Now I'd need to hide him under a brown paper wrapper. Who admits to reading titles like *Listen to the Warm*? Listen to the warm *what*? I wonder if he's still alive. Some Googling confirms he is, but his appearances are limited to autograph signings. This makes sense, since Amazon lists most of his books from a penny to $3 or so.

One section that should be easy to trim is business management. I'm tossing everything with the words "Excellence" or "Minute" in the title. I learned long ago that when it comes to business, it's far better to under promise and over deliver. Ditto on trimming the "How To" section, where I'll toss everything with "Dummy" or "Idiot" in the title. I don't need to be reminded of my self image when I bought them.

Ah! Here's a group I should be able to thin out—foreign language and travel. I pick up one that I don't remember; it's a street and transportation guide to Paris. It's so detailed it includes a section on one-way streets. The book was published in 1977. In all likelihood those *Sens Unique* are four lane roads today. For those who are wondering, *Sens Unique* is not French for psychic powers. The most use I'd get out of this book at this point in my life is as toilet paper. It's better quality than what was nailed to the stall walls the last time I saw Paris.

I should really get rid of most of the pocket sized dictionaries, but they take up so little room. You never know when you might be called upon to translate something into Latin. At the very least, I should get rid of the guides for any countries that require more than two immunization shots. At my age, I'll travel only to places that have flush toilets and pouffy duvets.

I expect to cut back a lot of the section on doll collecting, toys and miniatures. Then I remember that four of those stacked a certain way in two piles are exactly the right height to lift a box fan set on the washstand high enough for the breeze to pass over the footboard of the bed. Since I can't remember which four and I don't know if I'll have central air where we retire to, I'll need to keep all of them.

Those books on collectibles are thick suckers, as are my many art books. I remember the comment of someone I had coerced into helping me move to a new apartment many years ago. As he was lugging yet another pile of books to the van, he asked, "Do you buy your books by the pound?"

The answer of course was "no." But when I consider the cost of relocating our household, I just might get rid of some books based on how much they weigh. Suddenly those thin little Rod McKuen books are looking like keepers after all. Maybe I'll even get them autographed. Or not.

# More on Thinning Out the Closet

Original Post Date Oct.13, 2010

Some who have read my earlier post on thinning out my many closets have asked what happens if I still have too much left after I "audition" my clothes. I have new criteria to address that inevitable situation.

The first came to me last weekend as yet another woman complimented the handbag I was carrying. It's small white leather, with delicate painted flowers; the handles are yellow. I get frequent compliments on it, and I always share the story of how I lusted after it in a local Marshall's store, but wouldn't pay the price. One day I went in and it appeared that the bag had been sold. I found it tucked away in a far corner, on sale. I end this part by crying out *"It was meant to be mine!"*

Last weekend I was sure the bag shouted to the woman: *"Please stop complimenting her! She'll never give me up. I'm not supposed to be owned by a woman in her sixties. I belong with someone in her twenties!"*

This led to my first two rules for clearing out more stuff.

> *Rule 1: Keep things people always compliment, unless they fail rule two.*

*Rule 2: Get rid of anything that should be owned by someone in her 20's instead of her 60's, no matter how comfortable it is and no matter how cute I think I look in it. That's why God invented mirrors...*

One of my previous posts* prompted a guideline to keep a good balance of serious and light hearted. Some examples: a good interview suit—just in case—and a funeral outfit—also just in case, and the interview suit doesn't count, balanced by a gypsy-style skirt and a jacket with Guatemalan embroidery; and sensible black pumps, offset by red Chinesey platform slides.

I'll get rid of things that are major magnets for cat hair and will trash any sweaters that have more than three moth holes, even if they're well-darned. Anything that is no longer its original color gets tossed—except the white "Crazy Cat Lady" sleep T-shirt my brother-in-law gave me that is now pale turquoise. Likewise anything missing a button, if those buttons would cost more to replace than what I paid for the item.

I'll part with any shoes with buckles so small that I need a jeweler's loupe to fasten them, but I'll keep footwear that makes me smile when I look at my feet—especially my oxblood Doc Martin Mary Janes and my black patent duck-style rain shoes.

I'll give away any article of clothing that has writing on it—unless that writing is in French; all T-shirts will be exempt. Those of you who have been reading carefully will realize that the Crazy Cat Lady sleep shirt escapes the winnowing process even though it has writing on it, because it's an over-sized T.

You should also not be surprised that I'm keeping that little white purse with the flowers. Even though it fails rule two, I'm saving it from exile because it provides the light-hearted balance to my serious black shoulder bag.

If you know me well, you probably now have an image of me sitting on our front porch, wearing that Cat Lady shirt and holding my flowered purse. People will whisper as they walk by, but I'll just sit there quietly sipping a glass of wine. The more I think about it, I really am looking forward to retirement!

* See Serious vs. Lighthearted in Retirement Planning Section.

# Clearing the Kitchen and Pantry

Original Post Date Oct. 20, 2010

I'm not much of a cook, but I expect to do more of it after I retire. In preparation, I'm clearing out the kitchen and pantry to see which items are worth keeping. I'm finding things that haven't seen the light of day since they made the move with me 18 years ago. To get started, I set out storage boxes labeled "Donate," "Keep" and "Now What?"

With my kitchen foray, I've developed a theory that you can tell when someone was married by the wedding gifts they received. For my first marriage, we received at least three fondue pots during the decade of *"Do you fondue?"* (Did you?) Two of them turned up on the top shelf in the butler's pantry—one for cheese, one for beef cubes. I can't remember when I last used either of them. Gobs of melted cheese. Deep fried red meat. Cholesterol. Need I say more? I move both fondue pots to the Donate box.

There are countless cheese boards, so per my wedding gift theory, I married in the '80's, but I didn't—either time. Cheese boards must be like picture frames—the universal wedding gifts that transcend time and styles. Whatever the reason, though I use as many as three of them at a time for holiday entertaining, I need to get rid of some cheese boards.

I put six in the "Now What?" box and change the label on it to read "Re-Gift."

I also have more salad bowls than I need. The large stainless one and the wooden one get regular use, so they're keepers. The glass one with the silver-plated rim was a gift. Re-Gift. The plastic one matches all that picnic ware I bought and used once. Will we picnic when we're retired? Keep, just in case. These hand-painted pasta serving bowls can also be used for salads. Keep, Keep, Keep.

One of my miscalculations is a mini crock pot that goes into the microwave so it cooks faster. My microwave is called the Half Pint; that's not just a clever nickname—it's close to its capacity. The mini crock doesn't fit in it. Even if I have a standard microwave in our next abode, I'm as likely to be crock potting as fonduing. Into the Donate box it goes.

Be still my heart—it's a pull-out shelf full of Corningware, the new bride's best friend. I have everything from serving-sized bowls with plastic covers for leftovers to huge casserole-sized ones that are missing their glass lids. I rarely use any of it, but retirement may change that. Sorting through all of this will be a project in itself. I find another storage box, put back the label "Now What?" and fill it with Corningware.

Another shelf has been hiding a similar trove of Tupperware. Pie holder—Donate; my mother was the baker; I can never compare, so why try. Iceberg lettuce holder—Donate; I've moved on to romaine and it won't fit. Some sort of cheese or pound-sized butter holder—Donate; I have one that holds a single stick; I don't need to encourage milk fat consumption. All the Tupperware has been dispatched, but I don't feel smug; I know there's another shelf with Ziploc bowls and used deli containers that still need sorting.

My Donate box still has a lot more room. I wonder if there's a show like The Biggest Loser, but for people who need to get rid of stuff, not pounds. I could use someone like Jillian to be my tough-as-nails coach. *"Don't you dare put that in your Keep box! It's Donate or the trash or you'll never reach your goal. You can do it! Focus. Lift. Push."*

I'm exhausted just thinking about it. I need a glass of wine and a snack. I grab a cheese board from the top of the Re-Gift box. Hmmm… This is kind of cute—just right for one serving. Maybe I should keep it.

Jillian is shouting something vile at me, but I turn off my mental TV, lean back and relax. I carefully stack slices of artisanal cheese onto gluten-free crackers. Who says I don't know my way around the kitchen?

# Getting Down to Nothing
Original Post Date May 4, 2011

As most of you know, the last few weeks have been focused on getting rid of 18 years of clutter in the house. You've probably heard me mention that it's like the loaves and the fishes. As of last weekend, I wouldn't say I was feeling smug, but I was definitely feeling satisfied that I was making progress. Then came Sunday.

Sunday is the big day for open houses. I go to a few each week to get a sense of what the competition will be for my house when it's finally listed. An open house can also provide some ideas for staging. The two things any good real estate agent will likely tell me are: focus on curb appeal and get rid of the clutter.

Those who are in my house on any regular basis will attest that over the past few weeks I've made significant progress decluttering. But I'll bet that any realtor worth her commission would ask me when I plan to start clearing out stuff. This was driven home to me in spades after I went through the houses that were open last weekend.

I came home and sank into a deep funk. The two houses most comparable to mine had not one thing on their kitchen counters. Nothing. The only reason you can't write messages in the dust on my counters is that they're so covered with stuff you can't get at them.

I set about packing my cookbooks, which were gobbling up much of the counter real estate. Many of you are shocked that I own any cookbooks, given that I never cook. There's a reason I don't. My husband is so attached to his store that we rarely have dinner together. There's not a lot of *Joy of Cooking for One*, no matter what Irma Rombauer says. Since I expect more family dinners once we downsize to Vermont, I'm keeping most of the cookbooks.

After the books were packed and I'd cleaned the aforementioned dust, I surveyed the counter. On a relative basis, it looked great, but it was a far cry from being clear. This propelled me into one of my philosophical musings. Well, to be accurate, this plus a glass of *Chianti Classico*.

The point of those pristine counters is to present a metaphorical *tabula rasa* to a potential buyer. The message is that the house is a clean slate, awaiting the new beginnings of your family, dear buyer. Just imagine what you could imprint onto this space!

While I can appreciate this from a marketing perspective, I still have to live in the house while it's on the market. I must admit that, as I sit in the rooms that have been thinned out considerably, I feel a certain calm that my previously-cluttered style did not offer. I'm sure there's some *feng shui* operating here.

After awhile, I begin to feel like a stranger in my own home. There is a difference between calming and comforting. My home has always been my cocoon. Pictures of extended family used to crowd the horizontal spaces in most rooms. These are now all packed away. It occurs to me that I've lost my visual "comfort food."

This is somewhat surprising, when you consider that I used to look at the group photo of my aunts and think: *"Please, God, don't let me grow up to look like Aunt Lucrezia."* Now that she's in a box in the basement, with other beloved relatives who have long ago shed their mortal coil, I miss her. She is, after all, family. My family.

Realtors will pressure you into getting rid of all evidence that you have a family, with little regard to what this might do to your psyche. Fie on them! They have me torn between aggressively pursuing the perfectly staged house and preserving at least some token evidence that this is still my home.

I guess there's really only one way to solve this dilemma, and that's to open another bottle of Chianti. *Alla famiglia!* Especially Aunt Lucrezia.

# Getting to D-Day

Original Post Date May 25, 2011

Today was D-day on my plans to downsize and sell our house. I met with the first group of realtors that I'm interviewing to decide where I'll list. Since I've been attending a lot of open houses in my area as part of my "intelligence gathering," I knew that the current trend is to strip the house to the architectural equivalent of its underwear. Turns out, they really want it to be in its birthday suit.

I've been decluttering and packing and labeling for weeks. But unless you saw the house before I started, you'd have no idea how much has been removed. I've been operating on the *"s - - t flows downhill"* premise. That is, I started on the third floor and moved all of its excess down to the next level or lower. Eventually, everything deemed expendable found its way to the basement, where one room has been turned into what looks like a bomb shelter after the explosion.

Today's tag team of realtors told me to keep on decluttering and pack up my dolls. I have an antique doll collection. Some are displayed in glass cases; some are posed in children's and doll's furniture. I got a reprieve on the ones that are encased. I assume that once the others have been packed away, there will be no reason to keep their empty furniture on display.

Part of the agents' rationale for this is that I'm going to have to pack it all up when I move anyway. True. I'm also going to have to pack up my husband's Jockey shorts, but that doesn't mean I expect him to go commando for the next few months.

Perhaps it's just the contrarian in me, but I don't understand the psychology of convincing someone this is a house their family will want to make into their home by pretending the people living here now have not made it theirs. The open houses that are professionally staged appear sterile. Or, as I like to put it, they look like the house has had a lobotomy.

I'd much rather look at a house that has some warmth, that seems lived in. We're not in ancient Sparta, after all. And I'd like it to have a little more personality than Jack Nicholson did at the end of *"One Flew Over the Cuckoo's Nest."* Besides, how many people really want to be able to roll a bowling ball down their kitchen counter top anyway?

Don't get me wrong. I know you have to leave some things to the imagination. And I understand that pictures of our entire extended family can be a distraction. I packed them up long ago. Well, most of them. I have one picture of each of our closer relatives still on display. That adds up to about a dozen, but they're interspersed with other items on a wall full of built in bookcases.

I'm willing to pack up those family photos, too, if I'm forced to do so. But if you think I'm packing up the ones of my deceased cats, or rolling the custom made pottery jars with their ashes downhill to the basement bomb shelter, think again. There are some things that are just non-negotiable.

I'd sooner put away my wine rack, and you know how likely that is to happen. Speaking of which, I think it's time to sit back with a nice glass of Italian red. After all, dear Scarlet, tomorrow is another day. And another real estate agent is coming in the morning. Can't wait.

# Signs of Staging
Original Post Date Jun. 11, 2011

Our house is nearing L-day, the day it will be listed for sale as part of our plans to downsize. My Realtors provided a stager and I'm working my way through the long list of what he wants done before we can put the house on the market.

Many of them make sense—we all know we need to declutter and pack up all those family photos. But some items shout *"professional staging."* In celebration of the almost-completion of this process, here are the top ten signs a professional stager has prepped your house for sale.

10. All the towels in your bathrooms are white, but none of your bathrooms are. And by the way, they are unwashed, so they're still fluffy, and Lord help anyone who tries to actually use them.

9. All your toilet brushes and plungers are stowed out of sight. You've made notes of where they are because… well, out of sight out of mind, and at this point, you've totally lost yours.

8. Mr. Popper's penguins could now hold their bowling tournaments on your kitchen counter tops.

Provided they cleaned up after themselves when they were done.

7. There is not one single paperback on any of the 100 linear feet of built-in bookshelves in your house. Ditto for the 25 linear feet of shelving in various furniture items.

6. The carpeting in several rooms is now two different colors, in distinct rectangular patterns. To make the rooms look bigger, you had to get rid of several large pieces of furniture that had been in place for 18 years. Who remembered the original carpet color was deep blue, not faded slate?

5. All of the energy efficient helix light bulbs have been replaced with old-fashioned round ones, because incandescent light is more flattering to what is left of your décor.

4. The storage room in your basement looks like one of those little second-hand furniture sheds along a New England roadside. All it needs is a sign: "Ye Olde Curiosity Shoppe," and an elderly dog that smells like wet upholstery.

3. Your cats need psychiatric counseling because most of their favorite places to curl up have been banished

to that basement room. It's where they'll also be banished when the house is being shown. When that happens, they'll be glad their baskets and condos are down there.

2. Your husband can't find any of his favorite things. If the house doesn't sell quickly, he may need counseling, too. Or a basket in the basement storage room.

And the number one sign that a professional stager has prepped your house for sale:

1. You come back from one last staging errand and discover that your house keys no longer fit the locks.

# Kitchen Redo

Original Post Date Jun. 15, 2011

It's 7:30 on Wednesday evening and I'm waiting patiently for some inspiration for today's post. Once again, I have nothing. To be fair, I've been tied up this week with painters and plasterers. In between that, I was roaming the aisles of Home Depot, part of the time with my stager, part of the time by myself. More on that below.

My Realtor felt strongly—just one notch below "insisted"—that I needed to redo my kitchen. Not a done-done redo; just a freshening up. That meant removing old wallpaper, plastering, sanding, prepping and painting. Did I mention the ceiling was also wallpapered? We took the coward's way out and covered it with wallboard. Does that make it ceiling board? The ceilings are high so we could afford to lose a few inches.

I, too, can afford to lose a few inches, but I've yet to reap any weight reduction benefits from all my lifting and climbing. The only things I have to show for my hard work are black and blue marks up and down the insides of my arms. They're about three inches too short to effectively hold a carton of books without having to clutch them to my chest as though they were a case of my favorite wine. Or any wine, for that matter.

Back to the workers in my kitchen. It's mind boggling how much plaster dust one room can generate. No matter how careful the workmen are, it migrates throughout the house. They finished at 6:30 this evening and dutifully cleaned up the kitchen area and the front hall. I'm left to clean up the dust in the dining room, living room, back pantry and various other hallways and areas. As you might expect, writing this post seemed like a far more attractive task at this hour.

The kitchen certainly looks refreshed, or as I prefer to say, sterilized to within an inch of its life. If you look up *"tabula rasa"* in Wikipedia next week, you will likely see photos of my kitchen. (They have not yet been taken.) The only things between the redone room and Realtor perfection are that there is no hardware on the cabinetry and there are no overhead lighting fixtures.

Here is where my trips to Home Depot come into the story. My stager wanted me to replace the non-descript white porcelain knobs previously on the cabinetry with non-descript satin nickel knobs. Apparently, satin nickel is the material *du jour*. Moreover, the drawers will not get knobs, as they had before, but rather bin pulls. Picture an orange wedge, with the juicy part removed, and dipped in metal. You have a bin pull.

In addition, my knobs were in the wrong place. Oh, the ignominy! They should be in the bottom corner of the door. Mine were four inches too high. My cabinets are oversized, so the distance from the top of the door to the knobs was probably correct, but apparently that doesn't count.

I know I shouldn't take this personally. After all, the knobs were there when I bought the house in 1992. Still, I had an overwhelming urge to cross my arms over my chest when I heard: *"Your knobs are in the wrong place."* I should be grateful that the next sentence was: *"They're too high,"* rather than: *"They're half way to your knees."* My new knobs will be installed on Friday. Don't hold your breath waiting for photos.

Also on Friday, the new lighting fixtures will be put up. My old ones looked "too eighties." I didn't tell the stager that I actually purchased them in the nineties. In the first place, he wouldn't have let me keep nineties either. More importantly, I didn't want to admit that I purchased eighties lights in the nineties and didn't even realize it. Worse yet, I paid full price. How lame is that.

The good news is that my kitchen will now be *trés* 2011, or twenty-tens, or whatever we call the decade that we're currently in. The bad news is that we don't dare eat in it, cook in it, clutter it, or use it in any way. Now I understand why all those houses that have been professionally staged have kitchens with nothing in them. You move everything out so the workmen can have at it. Then you just don't move anything back in when they're finished.

I shudder to think what will happen if the Realtor takes a closer look at our bedroom. If the kitchen is any indication, we'll be banished from our own bed. I wonder if Home Depot sells air mattresses...

# Plain Vanilla Staging

Original Post Date Jun. 22, 2011

By now, those who have been following my rants know that it's my contention that the Plain Vanilla school of staging is not the optimum way to market a 100-plus year old Victorian. I now have some ammunition from the retail arena to support my case.

It comes from one of my frequent sources of inspiration, the *New York Times*. And let us not forget that even "the gray lady" added some color years ago. A June 15, 2011 article by Stephanie Clifford on retail mannequins made a claim that immediately caught my eye. *"The generic white, hairless, skinny mannequin is being pushed aside by provocative alternatives that entice shoppers."*

*"Aha!"* (said I). *"She has just described my repainted and staged kitchen. Generic white. Hairless and skinny."* I commented to some friends that a potential buyer who sees several properties staged by the same team will get confused about which kitchen was which. Here's a clue: mine is the one without granite counter tops.

I guarantee that a large percentage of homes on the market in Providence have kitchens painted Fossil and White Dove.

Likewise hardware in brushed nickel, and very likely my same new chandelier. I would be snorting up my sleeve after being shown three houses with identical plain vanilla décor.

More importantly, the potential buyer who is drawn to this décor is (IMHO) likely someone who really wants a new house. People who like Victorian houses are drawn to their character and charm. Staging a Victorian in plain vanilla is hiding its light under a bushel basket. Or in my case, inside a packing box in the basement.

Let's get back to Ms. Clifford and her report on the trend in retail mannequins, which she describes as *"a new apprecia-tion for old-fashioned window dressing."* Take that, stagers! So much for naked windows. Retailers are using mannequins to *"personify their brand"* and focus on a specific customer. That's what I feel staging should do for a house, especially one that has distinctive architecture.

It all comes down to Marketing 101. The seller shouldn't do things that will alienate a large number of potential buyers. However, trying to appeal to everyone's taste runs the risk of having everyone like your house a little bit, but having no one fall in love with it. If you use period-appropriate touches—in my case Victorian—to target the buyers who are most likely to truly appreciate your house, aren't you more likely to find a match?

Let me illustrate my point with descriptions of two types of mannequins—one from the seventies and one from today. In the 1970's, retailers kept costs down with generic mannequins that had no wigs and no make up. Bald and nondescript—in other words: plain vanilla.

Today, one designer store has mannequins that lie down, per Ms. Clifford, *"to help shoppers imagine wearing lingerie."* A professional stager would be shocked. *"What? Suggest that they should wear something specific? What if they don't want lingerie?"* Hello-o-o! You're selling lingerie. If they don't want it, they should be shopping at Pottery Barn.

Some of these new mannequins even have muscles. That's tantamount to putting color on a wall in the house. My stager would have apoplexy. He feels white walls let the buyer use her imagination about how she would decorate. I think he gives buyers too much credit. He's also out of touch with how busy women are.

Most of us would be happy to be handed a home that has tastefully colored walls, ones that are relatively neutral, but not plain vanilla. It saves us hiring a decorator. Excuse me. An interior designer.

I'm having one of Oprah's "Aha!" moments, the ones where a light bulb goes off above your head. I think I've stumbled upon the real reason that stagers want everything done in vanilla. As my mother would have said, they're in cahoots with the interior designers. By having houses done all plain, it forces the buyers to hire designers to add character to the interior of their shell of a new home.

So, the seller—or the seller's real estate agent—pays the stager to clear out every vestige of décor from the home. The buyer then hires the stager's partner—legal or unofficial—to redo the décor. If there is any justice in this world, the interior designer attends the seller's tag sale and buys most of the décor the seller was forced to dispose of. It then winds up back in the house where it started out.

Is this a great country, or what?

# Name That Paint Color
### Original Post Date Jul. 9, 2011

By now you must have read at least one of my posts bemoaning the lack of character in the paint colors my Realtor and her stager had me use in my kitchen. They want everything to be as neutral as possible, so we don't alienate anyone. As a marketer, I feel we're missing the opportunity to engage our key target audience—someone who will appreciate turn of the century architecture.

One of my go-to sources for posting ideas had an article that offers a compromise. In the June 30, 2011 *New York Times*, Katharine Q. Seelye wrote about how paint companies are changing the way they name their colors. Per Ms. Seelye, they're doing this to capture consumers' attention. They're now using names that, among other things, *"summon a memory or evoke an emotion"* or represent the consumer's lifestyle. The names rarely have any relationship to the colors they represent, and it's OK if they sound negative.

I smell a marketer behind this trend! Home Depot's merchandising VP for paint articulated my compromise nicely when she stated that *"Emotional color names in neutral shades and color combos are crucial for successful home sales."* Thank you, Lyne Castonguay. Since my house painting is now complete, it's left to me to come up with emotional names for what are mostly bland, unemotional colors.

Let's start with the kitchen, which has been painted Fossil (walls) and White Dove (cabinets and trim.) I'm naming this combination *"Truffle Season in Piemonte."* My sister and her husband took his sister and me there during truffle season. The weather was overcast, so the vistas were a hazy, grayish white. That's also the color of white truffles as they are shaved onto your risotto. While my potential buyer is mentally savoring truffles in Piemonte, perhaps she won't notice the lack of granite countertops and designer appliances.

The entry hall and stair tower have mostly bittersweet orange and white striped wallpaper. It's subtle, as stripes go, but it runs on and on up three stories in the tower. If it were a color, what comes to mind for me is *"On Hold for the Social Security Office."*

The living room is wallpapered light blue with pale coral medallions. If it were a color, it would be *"Quiet Walk on the Beach at Sunrise."* There's even a Coalport china bowl filled with sea shells on the sideboard.

The dining room has been painted a spicy color that borders on neutral. I'm calling this *"Learning to Do the Tango."* That should highlight the open spaces in the entry and dining areas; there's room enough to tango.

The master bedroom has muted wallpaper with soft sprigs of flowers. It gives the impression of being painted cream, as in *"Homemade Eggnog at Our Tree Trimming Party."*

The main guest bedroom has been painted Parchment, but I'll call it *"Love Letters from Your First Boyfriend."* That should make buyers notice the bay window with its romantic seating area. The smaller guest room has nondescript wallpaper—off white with fine blue plaid lines. I'll name this *"Pedal Pushers You Wore to Band Camp."* Don't ask.

The third floor bedroom that is newly painted is pale yellow (Lemon Whip) and the bathroom is pale green (Green Tea.) I'm renaming them *"Remember When Whole Foods Was Bread and Circus"* and *"Lunching with Friends at Whole Foods."* There are two Whole Foods within two miles of us, lest we forget; reason enough to buy the house just for that.

I haven't named the colors in every room, but I feel that I've covered the ones that will matter most to my target audience. If my office area weren't paneled in faux wood, I'd color it *"Where I Go with My Glass of Wine When I Need Inspiration."*

Speaking of which, here I am at my computer. Now if I can just remember where I moved the wine when the stager banished it from the dining room...

# St. Joseph the Realtor

Original Post Date Aug. 20, 2011

Those of you who follow me on other on-line fora will know by now that the deal to sell my house has fallen apart. Not one to be deterred by a bump in the road, I'm taking action to find another, better buyer. To wit, we are taking the first price markdown next week, and I've just come in from burying a statue of St. Joseph in my front yard.

A few of you out there look perplexed. Let me explain. There is a long standing (sub)urban myth that burying St. Joseph upside down in your yard will help you sell your house. It's unclear why he must be upside down. Is he really likely to wander off (under ground) if upright?

I considered burying him sideways, like a ship in a bottle, but in an empty *Pinot Noir*. I guess the notion of "sideways" reminded me of the terrific movie of that title, the one that had a stream of *Pinot* running through it.

You probably think of St. Joseph as Jesus's carpenter father. Or perhaps as the inventor of children's aspirin. It's unclear how he came by his role as real estate sales facilitator. It was probably some extension of carpentry and building.

This of course makes me wonder if he is as effective selling brick houses as wood ones. Fortunately for me, my home is good old New England clapboard. It's pronounced "clabberd" up here, by the way, not "clap-board." True New Englanders also spell the old nursery rhyme mother "Hupboard."

Another possibility for how St. Joe got into real estate sales is that it's one big headache, especially for the seller. Before Excedrin, aspirin would have been the drug of choice to deal with this. Today, there's Vicodin, but I don't think it has a saint endorsing it yet.

However it came about, the notion of burying St. Joseph upside down has so many proponents that you can buy little kits, complete with instructions. Mine came courtesy of my Realtor. Here's what I learned from the material that was included.

There are several acceptable places to bury the statue. These include by your doorstep (facing away), near the street (facing the house) and by the Realtor's sign (no advice re which way to face; read into that what you will).

I've opted for the doorstep approach. It will be easier to tell if the squirrels have dug it up, mistaking it for a plant bulb.

The advice is clear as to the depth to bury it—8 inches, not 3 feet. No arguments from me on that. I have trouble getting to one foot when I'm gardening. These and several other tidbits are bulleted neatly on the back of the instruction card.

Below the bullets, there's a paragraph that advises that St. Joseph's power lies in the prayers you say to him and how faithful you are in your devotion. A separate prayer card is provided. I had been wondering how the Catholic Church could countenance this practice, but the focus on the prayers answered that.

Next is the sentence that makes me sit up physical-therapy-straight and take notice. *"You can also increase your chance of selling your home by making sure it is in good condition and by asking a realistic price."* Spoken like a true Realtor. Then I notice that the section with the bullet points is titled "How-To-Myths" while the paragraph below them is titled "The Truth." This must be the liability disclaimer. I can hear it now:

> *"I buried the statue and nothing happened. I want my money back."*
>
> *"Did you pray daily?"*
>
> *"Well, not exactly…"*
>
> *"Um hmmm. And was your home in good condition and did you price it realistically?"*
>
> *"Let's put it this way. It never looked as good as when I first put it on the market. The price seemed realistic when my Realtor and I first sat down with comps."*

*"And what about three weeks later, when the stock market tanked and Congress went home for summer recess?"*

*"Yeah, well, maybe you have a point."*

*"You might want to try burying two more statues of St. Joseph in the other locations we suggested. We have a buy-one-get-one-half-off promotion going on now."*

*"Won't that give him an identity crisis?"*

*"Not if you pray at each statue individually..."*

And that, dear readers, is why I put one of my bottles of *Pinot Grigio* into the fridge before I started writing this. It just so happens that I had two of them in my wine cupboard—one for each of the promotional St. Joes.

The Lord does indeed work in strange ways...

*Saint Joseph
the Realtor®*

# Section III

# Retirement Planning

# Drawing a Line in the Sand

Original Post Date Sep. 3, 2010

A big part of the retirement process is deciding exactly when you should retire. Most of the things I've seen written about this have to do with finances—figuring out your "number" (how much you'll need to live on).

I spent—and continue to spend—a fair amount of time running numbers. What will be my expenses if I do it now, if I live there instead of here? What will be my income, Social Security in particular, if I go on this date vs. that? Figuring out what I'm likely to get for the house when I downsize. Re-figuring what I'll get for the house as the real estate market goes into the toilet. And re-figuring yet again when someone or something pulls the "flush" handle.

You hear people talk about their "full" retirement age. But I see Social Security as a continuum. Retire a few months early and you get a little less. Hang on a few months longer and you get a little more. You don't really max out until 70. A few months from "full" one way or the other makes very little difference.

What finally prompted me to draw a line in the sand and pick a date to retire had very little to do with money and very much to do with emotions. One of my closest friends died two years ago of lung cancer. She was a few years younger than I, and far more physically fit. And she'd never smoked a day in her life. By the time the doctors figured out what was wrong, she was stage four. They gave her 5 weeks, but she was with us 5 months.

That was a real wake up call for me. I realized that we never really know how much time we have left. I decided that as soon as I could put the pieces together enough to keep the wolves away from the door, I would retire. I'll be dragging my husband—who is 11+ years my senior—kicking and screaming from his self-owned place of business. If it were up to him, he'd work forever. I figure I'll be doing him a favor.

I drew that line in the sand for us at the end of this year (2010). We have our eyes set on Northern Vermont, where my sister and her family live. Instead of seeing them just once or twice a year, we'll be close enough to visit regularly. I'll get to "do lunch" with my sister. I'll get to go shopping with my niece, who is like the daughter I never had. I'll get to watch my grandniece, who was a micro-preemie, grow up.

And instead of wishing I had time to write (my secret passion), I'll be doing it every day, as many hours as I'd like. Speaking of which, today is Day 3 of my blog. I like to think of it as getting in shape for when I retire.

# Spiffing Up the Yard—
# The Lawn as Metaphor

Original Post Date Sep. 8, 2010

A key step in my plans to downsize the house after I retire is to get the outside looking its best. We all know the two mantras of every real estate agent: "location, location, location" and "curb appeal." I selected our home back in 1992 with location in mind, and the neighborhood has held up nicely. I wish I could say as much for our yard.

Last fall I had major repairs made to the house's exterior and had it painted. This summer I've been working on spiffing up the yard. I have a service that does weed and grub control, liming, etc. I just contracted to have them aerate the lawn and over-seed it in October.

As I push the mower around, I can feel that the terrain is treacherous. There are lumps and bumps under my feet. It looks like a training ground for baby gophers. There are no actual holes, but some of the indentations are almost as dangerous.

As I made the decision that my lawn needs a wider array of professional services, it occurred to me that it's a metaphor for our hair as we age. Overall, it's a lot thinner than it was in years past. Like my husband's head these days, it has a lot of bald spots. The crabgrass reminds me of my own hair on many occasions—wild and out of control and sticking up in all directions. Large portions of it still have good color, but some areas are so faded, they're almost colorless.

As I mulled over this metaphor and looked around the entire yard, I started thinking about the rest of our bodies as we approach retirement. The sidewalks, with cracks and discolorations here and there, were suddenly like skin in areas exposed to years of sun. I saw small clumps of grass/hair sprouting in places they don't belong and bushes that could use trimming.

Who would have thought than an assessment of my house's curb appeal could lead to a cold, hard look into the mirror of self-reflection? That's OK. There are professionals out there who offer services that can improve MY curb appeal, too.

Note to self: increase 'Personal Expenses" line in retirement budget.

# Fine-tuning the Budget
Original Post Date Sep. 11, 2010

An essential step in retirement planning is to prepare a realistic budget. I've been tracking my expenditures for years using a spreadsheet I created myself. Its original purpose was to help me at tax time. I therefore didn't obsess about where to log items that weren't deductible. Now that I'm inching toward retirement, I need to figure out where I can cut back. That requires thinking more carefully about how I categorize everything I spend.

Let's take for example how I account for wine. I currently log it under entertainment. After all, it has no nutritional value. Entertainment happens to be a category where I expect to cut back. Although I share much of the wine with friends or dinner guests, sometimes I drink alone. That begs the question: Should the wine I drink by myself get logged under "personal"? Don't get that "I understand, dear" look on your face. A glass or two gives me inspiration for my writing, which will be my profession in retirement. Come to think of it, does that mean I can claim it as a business expense?

What about cat food? Currently, I log that under groceries; it's all on one receipt so that makes it easier. I suppose it really belongs under "cat care/vets." What about the food I give to the neighbors' cats that beg at our door? Doesn't it properly belong in "gifts"? That's another category where I plan to cut back. If one of the cats turns out to be a stray, can his food be claimed as "charity"?

The personal category is another one that bears scrutiny. Much of what goes in there is hair coloring and haircuts, both of which are now on a five-week schedule. If I switch to a six-week schedule, I'll reduce that expense by about 17%. Even after we've retired to Vermont, I plan to keep seeing Jason here in Providence. When you've spent years finding and training a hairdresser, you don't give him up easily. That means I'll be driving from the Burlington area back to RI every time I need a cut. Shouldn't I post the gas for that trip under "personal"? This flies in the face of my plans to reduce that category. I have an idea! If I bring my husband with me so he can check on his store while I'm getting trimmed, I can deduct the trips as a business expense.

When I was in marketing at Colgate Palmolive, we had an expression that was popular at budget time: *"Figures don't lie; liars figure."* The fact is, I can configure my plan any way I want. That won't guarantee that the numbers will hold up. I had no idea budgeting for retirement could be so stressful.

I think I'll go open a bottle of wine, and since I'm doing it to deal with the stress, I'll log this one under "medical."

# Alcohol Really Is Medicinal

Original Post Date Sep. 15, 2010

Picking up where I left off in my September 11 post: I had concluded that the cost of wine I drink alone will be categorized as "medical" in my retirement budget. My rationale was that it helps me deal with stress. It turns out, I'm on the cutting edge of medical thinking.

A September 2010 issue of *Time* magazine reports on research that suggests that alcohol consumption extends your life. You read me right. A 20 year study of 1,824 people showed that 69% of teetotalers died during the study, while only 41% of moderate drinkers did. (Heavy drinkers fell in between, with 60% dying.) Don't panic. They were aged 55-65 when the study started.

These astonishing results led me to immediately increase my budgeted allocation for wine after I retire. The main reason I don't drink more now is that I'm usually the driver. When we're home more, I'll be able to imbibe more. Knowing that it's healthy is just added incentive, not to mention the possibility of a tax deduction.

Other ramifications of this study occurred to me as I read it a second time. The first was that I must get my husband on the *vino* wagon so that he'll have a 28% greater chance of living longer, too. Jagdish has a bad reaction to the preservatives in most wines, especially so-called "affordable" ones. However, his system tolerates the pricier wines that we usually have at holiday dinners with my sister Barbara's family. Since we'll be living near them in retirement, I foresee many more opportunities to enjoy the good stuff.

This of course means revising my wine budget still higher, even more so because I'm not as likely to be drinking alone. This is probably good news, since the researchers surmised that the social interactions that usually accompany drinking are a factor in maintaining good health. Flash forward to visions of my brother-in-law, Bob, and me, relaxing in side by side lounge chairs, cradling our shared bottle of Barolo. Barbara and Jagdish are reading nearby, looking far more dignified and far less in their cups.

My husband, the non-drinker, was unexpectedly very interested in this study. *"How do they define moderate?"* he asked. The answer was a surprising 1 to 3 glasses per day. He followed this with *"What size glass?"* I said I assumed a typical size for the drink being consumed.

What had me scratching my head was the "per day" part. I would have guessed "per week." If "1 to 3 glasses per day" is moderate, how much would I have to drink for it to be considered heavy?

The answer is immaterial. In order to afford even a moderate amount of good wine each day, I'll have to let my hair go gray and give up professional haircuts altogether. I decide this will be a small sacrifice to make. After all, I'm committed to improving my health after I retire. It also seems like the least I can do for my husband, my sister and my brother-in-law. I raise my wine glass: *Alla famiglia!*

# Adjusting to New Schedules
Original Post Date Sep. 22, 2010

I've never been a morning person. My preferred schedule is late to bed, late to rise., and I reach my creative peak around 2 am. Fortunately, my husband is also a night person. I need 8 to 9 hours of sleep to function at my best; Jagdish can make do on far fewer.

While my current job allows me some flexibility of start time, it's not enough for me to follow an ideal schedule. One of the things I look forward to in retirement is following my natural circadian rhythm.

Yet, when it comes to retired people I know, most of them go to bed early and get up even earlier. I wonder if this is an inevitable change that comes with retirement. Will the evenings of inspired writing that I look forward to not come to be after all?

As preparation for this transition, should I be trying to get to bed a little earlier each week and to rise earlier, too? I've read that adjusting sleep patterns is similar to dealing with jet lag—do it gradually, an hour at a time. Once I stop working, will I crawl into bed at 10 pm, or even 9, too tired to log on to my computer? Is this schedule change the inevitable destiny for the retiree? I can't bear to contemplate it.

A chilling thought occurs to me. We're probably going to retire to a condo in a development focused on seniors. Is it possible that the membership rules in these communities specify a curfew? Lights out by 11 pm. I envision the block captain as he pedals silently through the streets on a three-wheeled bike. Around his neck is a whistle on a macramé lanyard made by an 88 year old woman in the Wednesday morning craft club.

Stay up too late and he plasters a red sticker on your door that proclaims "Violation!" Oh the ignominy! Worse yet, they have circuit breakers up stream and they just cut your power. The only warning is three short blasts on the whistle, barely enough time to hit the "save" key. Of course, this is a ridiculous notion. Or is it? I have enough to worry about in my retirement planning without adding curfew police to the list.

As luck would have it, a news story in the latest *"Brown in the Media"* catches my eye. It reports on research showing that teenagers perform better when they are allowed to heed their "biological imperative." That is to stay up until at least 11 pm and then get 8 or more hours of sleep.

These findings led to some experiments to accommodate this schedule by having school start an hour or so later. The delayed starts corresponded with better grades and reduced obesity. Apparently, teens deal with drowsiness by shoveling in extra sweets.

No need to put this information in front of me twice. I have enough trouble controlling my weight without buying into a lifestyle change that feeds a junk food habit. If I have my druthers—and I certainly plan to have them after I retire—I'll heed my biological imperative, which seems to be stuck at the teenage level. Late to bed, late to rise. That should help me retain a youthful vigor. Cue the music: *"...forever young, I want to be forever young."*

Notes to self: Reconsider getting house instead of condo; buy blackout curtains.

# Greening Up the House
Original Post Date Oct. 16, 2010

As if the road to salvation weren't challenging enough, the Catholic Church added polluting to its list of mortal sins. That's right, Gianfranco Girotti, the Vatican official who heads up the B-team on confessions and penitence put contamination of the environment right up there with the seven deadly ones. No word on what the head of the A-team thinks of this, though I'm sure he'd agree with Girotti's postulate that "sin is social" in today's global culture.

I'm not exactly a poster child for green living. I've never even hugged a tree, unless you count my lame attempt to rescue one of our cats when she was still a kitten. Nonetheless, I find it irresistible to improve my chances of making it through the pearly gates by reducing my eco-footprint. There's the added benefit that greening up could shorten the time to sell our house when I retire. I read that home buyers are increasingly interested in how "green" a property is.

I resolve to become a cleaner, greener, holier (than thou) neighbor. My new mantra will be *"Reduce, Re-use, Recycle."* To get organized, I start two lists: "to do" and "to buy." My first "to do" as a born-again environmentalist is to locate my folder of dog-eared articles on conservation and the environment. It's a fat folder, one of many on a variety of topics I've researched. My previous mantra was *"If you can't recycle it, file it."*

First on my eco-agenda is something called xeriscaping—an approach to landscaping that minimizes water usage. This is a propitious discovery, since the timer on our sprinkler system died last season. I consider the options, given that the only lawn we have is in front of the house. *"Put a deck over the areas that get a lot of traffic."* That would be our entire yard and I've never seen a fully decked house-front on the East Side of Providence.

I rule out *"Cultivate plants that require minimal water."* If I planted beds of cacti around our Victorian, the garden police would be at my door before you could spell xeriscape. I decide that keeping our grass is not really a social sin, since our lawn has proved to be the most sociable place for the neighborhood dogs to do their business. I add a "to do": fix lawn sprinkler.

Next in my files on green technology is "geo-engineering." Scientists are planning to put enormous mirrors into orbit so they can bounce sunlight back into space, presumably to reduce global warming. As I gather information for constructing our "thousand points of light" cooling device, it occurs to me: our home is in a historic neighborhood. Construction not of the period (pre-1900 for us) is not allowed. I consult

McAlesters' *"Field Guide to American Houses."*
Surprisingly, roof mirrors are not included as identifying features for late 19th century styles. Yet another of my attempts to become greener has withered on the vine.

Increasingly frustrated and on the verge of panic, I add "Prozac refill" to my shopping list. Then I remember a leaflet someone stuffed in our front door years ago. It promoted greener alternatives to toxic cleaners and pesticides. I rummage through the kitchen drawer that every household has as its de facto filing cabinet and voila! I skim the section headings and pause on "Controlling Garden Pests." Maybe I can create a "green" exterior.

The leaflet advises me to *"promote beneficial pests such as fly larvae, aphids and thrips."* With all the holes the cats put in our screens, if I promoted fly larvae, I'd be scouring my supplemental insurance policy to see if it covers therapy. Aphids and thrips are two of the creatures I spray to get rid of. I'm skeptical that they can be their own natural predators, unless of course they have a primary system designed by the Democrats... Clearly this is another dead end on my path to salvation and a quick sale of our house.

With no more dog-eared files or leaflets, I remain a socially-challenged sinner. I realize I'm doomed. I am going to hell. I just hope it's in an eco-friendly hand basket.

# Spousal Adjustment

Original Post Date Oct. 30, 2010

My apologies to those of you who were lured to read this thinking it would be about sending your spouse off somewhere for a tune-up, hoping he or she would be returned performing more to your liking. This post would perhaps be more accurately titled *"How to Help Your Spouse Adjust to Your Retirement,"* but I like my headings short.

Regular readers of this blog know that I plan to downsize to Vermont soon after my retirement at year's end. A logical consequence of this is that my husband—who is eleven years my senior—will also semi-retire and move with me. Those who know Jagdish might call it an illogical consequence, since my husband is attached to the stool in his retail store by a virtual umbilical cord. This naturally raises concerns in my mind about how he'll adjust to "our" retirement.

The back story is that when we married 20 years ago, I gave up my friends and moved from my comfort zone in New Jersey to be with Jagdish in Providence. We agreed that our retirement move would be to the place of my choosing, which is near my family in northern Vermont. We've spent many holidays there and we both like that area. Our plan is for us to have side-by-side desks, where I'll write and he'll work on the website for his store, with my help.

This does not make me any less concerned about how my husband will adjust to the move. Ostensibly, his store sells clothing, jewelry, wind chimes, incense and all sorts of gifts. It's in a college community and his best selling item is the Schnoz tissue box in the shape of Shakespeare's face; the tissues dispense from—you guessed it—the bard's nose. It just occurred to me that this is ironic, since my husband shares the distinctive feature of many males in his family—an unusually large nose.

Spectrum India could easily be described as a bustling, colorful bazaar. However, one of my husband's friends was on point when he told him: *"You're not running a store; you're running an ashram."* From his stool behind the cash register, Jagdish dispenses not just change, but also advice. People call him "the guru of Thayer Street." He's a cross between a resident philosopher and Gertrude Stein, holding daily salons where people come to discuss the issues of the day. Or night, as he rarely closes before 1 AM.

On a one-on-one level, he also serves as a psychologist/counselor. He recently told me about someone who was sad, in part because she had no money to spend. This was his advice to her, probably given along with the gift of a peacock feather. A lot of the good things in life are free, so enjoy them. The air is free, at least until someone figures out how to put meters under our noses, so breathe deeply and more often. *[The image of a meter under Jagdish's nose made us both laugh.]*

His advice continued. Smiles release endorphins and serotonin, so smile all the time, even when you are sad; it will lift your spirits. Hugs increase the hormone oxytocin, and that makes you feel good and reduces stress. So find someone to hug each day. If you can't find someone else, then wrap your arms around to your back and hug yourself. *[I checked this out. He was reporting the results of an actual NIH study.]*

He even had a specific dosage for that last item, which he claims he heard somewhere, but it wasn't in the NIH study. You need 4 hugs a day to survive, 8 hugs for daily maintenance, and 12 to thrive. He hypothesized that too many hugs could cause an overdose of oxytocin. I have no doubt he gave the sad young woman four hugs before she went on her way.

Simple advice. Easy to follow. Delivered so earnestly and with such charm, that no one can resist him. So you see why I'm concerned about our pending relocation. I've suggested that Jagdish should bring his stool with him to Vermont. Perhaps there is a store like his own on Church Street in downtown Burlington. He can ask the owner to let him sit by the door, chatting and dispensing advice and philosophy. And maybe hugs.

If that doesn't work out, he can always just breathe deeply, smile and hug me. At least 12 times. With the hours he currently spends in his store, that's about 10 hugs more than we get to share now. With our luck, we'll get carried away and wind up institutionalized for a hug overdose. I have a vision of our therapy sessions—touching but no hugging. We are making molds of each other's faces to create customized Schnoz boxes. His are selling like hotcakes at Spectrum.

# Finding Stable Friends
Original Post Date Nov. 27, 2010

One of the challenges of retirement is finding new friends if you relocate. You might think this is not an issue for people who are reasonably outgoing. That depends on one's expectations for those new friends.

A few years back I titled the *"Philosophy Corner"* in my annual newsletter *"I'm Sorry If I Made You Fat."* I'd recently read the results of a study showing that if the people in your social circle were overweight, it was more likely you'd be, too. Now I've read an interview with a Brown professor who claims that the same is true about divorce. Simply put, if you want to stay married, pay close attention to the stability of the relationships of those around you.

So, in addition to looking for new friends with a sense of humor, reasonable intelligence and a taste for ethnic cuisine, we'll need to screen them for signs of a deteriorating relationship. I've come up with a handful of criteria that I believe will provide early warning signs that a partnership is doomed.

An obvious indication that things are not on solid ground: one of them has a divorce attorney on speed dial. If their prenuptial agreement is more than ten pages long, you can be pretty sure someone already had an exit strategy before walking down the aisle. They may as well have said "I do-ish" or "I might." Call me a skeptic, but I think a marriage is iffy for long term if either of the parties is on their third marriage. I know, I know. *"Third time's the charm."* But that can be said for divorce, too.

My screening criteria include some behavioral-based observations about long-term compatibility. For example, if one listens to NPR daily and the other shops regularly at WalMart, don't expect to be re-gifting that silver plated fruit basket you own for their twenty-fifth anniversary. Ditto when one is vegan and the other has a lifelong love affair with marbled red meat. There's no room for compromise in those diets, and a meat cleaver will outmaneuver a potato peeler any day.

Other signs of impending disintegration come with a retirement that required downsizing. Keep an eye out for trouble if they used to have separate bathrooms, but now they have to share one. Based on my personal experience, I'd give that couple a wide berth. One sign that you probably never considered: they retired to a condominium, but he refuses to give up his riding mower. One day, he'll head over yonder ridge and just keep going. You can afford a lot of gas for a mower, even at today's prices.

These criteria should help Jagdish and me weed out most of the potential new friends who could exert a negative influence on our marriage. What worries me more is if the ones who pass our test are conducting the same type of screening on us. I can hear them now. *"He seems nice enough, really mellow. But she's a bit intense, don't you think? How much longer do you figure they'll stay together?"*

Or maybe: *"He doesn't seem to give much thought to planning things, and she's obsessive about every detail—a classic Virgo. They'll never last." "Didn't he say he's allergic to most wine? But she sure seems to enjoy the fruit of the vine. Let's steer clear of that pair."*

So much for finding stable friends when we relocate. Now, where did I put that cork screw...

# A Shifting Line in the Sand
Original Post Date Dec. 1, 2010

My husband called me the other day with an idea for a RetirementSparks post. Someone told him the time was twenty-five minutes to three. My husband countered that it was actually two thirty-five. He saw this as a variation on the glass half full vs. empty question. Stated differently: Are you focused on the present—it's two thirty-five—or the future—twenty-five minutes to three? I'm guessing he sees the present as the half-full option here.

The retirement correlation seems to be: Do I have three more weeks left in my working life? Or am I three weeks away from retirement? Neither, as it turns out. As my presumed retirement draws closer, I expected my plans to be solidifying. Instead, they seem to be turning to jello. Put another way, that line that I drew in the sand a few months ago seems to be shifting from my reading glasses zone to my driving ones.

Some things at work have conspired to make it likely that I'll be working full time at least two or three more months. Or, futuristically—and glass half empty, that retirement will be two or three months away. The more I try to plan for retirement, the more I find myself questioning how to define it.

Although my first benchmark was eligibility for Medicare, that had more to do with when I might afford to retire, not when I planned to. Likewise, the date my pension from a former career maxed out helped define an earliest possible date.

Many people define retirement as when they stop working, preferably out of choice. For some that means no full time job; for others, it means not even part time work. I've always thought of "retirement" more as being able to stay up as late as I want every night and then sleep in, a time when I could spend my waking hours doing whatever I want. Or doing nothing. As if.

I suppose I could work part time and still qualify as semi-retired, using my own definition. That begs the question: "Is retirement a state of being or a state of mind?" If one's schedule says "retired," but one's head is still "showing up" at that mental office every morning, who's kidding whom? Likewise, if you come to work every day, but are counting the hours until the final punch out, aren't you effectively retired?

When the dust has settled (or the grains of sand), I suppose it doesn't really matter how you label the phase of life that comes for most of us sometime after age 65. And it's not really important exactly where we draw that line. What matters is how gracefully we navigate the passage. Of course, it would be nice to have a boat that's leak-free and to have at least one paddle. And a really good bottle of wine.

# Road Wanderers

Original Post Date Dec. 8, 2010

You've probably heard the phrase "road warriors," the business people—usually sales reps—who spend most of their time in their cars. Their vehicles are essentially traveling offices, complete with computers, phone/faxes, office supplies, samples of their wares, if appropriate, and the basic necessities for frequent overnight stays. It wouldn't surprise me if some of them even have minibars and yoga mats and Wii.

I think I've discovered their retirement equivalent: "road wanderers." Road wanderers spend their time traveling around in their cars, visiting family and friends that they likely have not seen for decades. I figured this out on my way back from a trip to the New York metro area this past weekend.

It began with the annual brunch my college friend, Dee Dee, arranged on Saturday. I opted to drive from Providence the evening before. As I took note of the rising cost of gas, I decided to combine some other visits with this trip. I stayed Friday night with my nephew, Barry, his wife, Meg, and their twins in Westport, CT. They'd moved there several months ago, but I hadn't seen their house yet.

Then I tacked on Saturday dinner in West Central Jersey with my former partner, Charlie, and his family from his first marriage. It was a slightly early birthday celebration for him, arranged by his daughter to coincide with my visit. Sunday midday I connected with a summer friend I hadn't seen in over 40 years. She found me on FaceBook. By coincidence, Ann, who lives near Philadelphia, was doing a puppet show five miles from where Charlie lives. If you're counting, that makes four connections.

Saturday night, I was supposed to be back in Connecticut staying with Lee, a former colleague from my corporate life, in anticipation of lunch on Monday. We were going to connect with Maida, another former colleague. Are you still with me? This all was canceled when Lee fell ill.

With Monday lunch—and friend tick-offs 5 and 6—no longer scheduled, I found myself driving home Sunday night, a day early. As I passed through the section of New Jersey where I went to high school, I thought, *"If I'd known I would have the evening free, I could have stopped off to see Ted and Ellen. They live quite near here."* Ted was one of my fellow band geeks. That's when it hit me: this could be a preview of my retirement years.

This got me to thinking about how I'd need to equip my car for life as a road wanderer. Certainly I'd need the ability to use a computer and a phone. I know what you're thinking.

Get Skype on the computer and you won't need the phone. Have you tried to set up Skype? Humor me on this one.

I'll need the ability to brew a proper cup of tea. Perhaps a mini-microwave. Does that mean I'd need a solar array on the roof of the car? I can't imagine being away from my cats for any length of time. So I'd need cat-friendly lounging and scratching areas for them. Then there's the litter...

Since I might not know how long I'd be away on each trip, I'd need a month's supply of all my medications. Oh, the paperwork! And vitamins. And lotions. And dental floss. It would also be helpful to have a book on B&Bs that allow cats and to have a Zagat's guide. There's nothing worse than wandering the Amish Country looking for a restaurant that specializes in South Indian food. Or having an unrequited longing for thin-crust pizza in Colonial Williamsburg.

You may have noticed that I did not mention a portable wine cellar. I'm careful not to have more than half a glass when I'll be driving. As a road wanderer, I'd likely have to give up the *vino* en route. Quite a sacrifice, now that I think about it.

No wine; lots of litter. Hours upon hours with my driving glasses pressing on the bridge of my nose, making those ugly red marks. I may have to go back to the drawing board on this idea. And as long as I'm passing by the wine rack on my way there...

# Warnings and Contraindications

Original Post Date Jan. 12, 2011

We're all familiar with the warnings and contraindications that come with various prescription drugs. They're required disclosures in TV ads. Some of them are so horrendous-sounding that it makes you wonder who would even consider taking the medications. What disease could be so bad that you'd sign on for bloating and diarrhea to treat it?

I think retirement should come with similar disclosures. It might cause us to think twice before doing it. After paying careful attention to TV ads for meds, I've developed a list of proposed language to accompany retirement proposals.

Warning: the loss of regular, sustainable income may lead to hostility and changes in mood. No longer having a place to go to work each day may cause depression and agitation and may lead to unprovoked arguments with anyone who is foolish enough to co-habit with you.

After dramatic change in your daily routine, you may have trouble sleeping and may have unusual dreams. These may be recurring dreams that border on nightmares. You may also experience bizarre changes in your daytime behavior, such as exercising to Jane Fonda's workout video while still wearing your pajamas, watching court TV and taking notes, and regularly emailing the co-hosts of *The View*.

Do not operate heavy machinery if you are angry over the fact that your IRA investments have gone straight down the toilet. Heavy machinery includes automobiles, vacuum cleaners, laundry equipment and coffee makers. In other words, don't even bother getting out of bed until you calm down.

Concerns over the stability of Social Security may lead to shortness of breath, difficulty thinking, the inability to focus and can inhibit your basic ability to function as a productive member of society. These side effects are usually, but not always, temporary (i.e. may improve in five to ten years.)

Do not retire if you have ever experienced nausea or had even a slight alcohol-induced buzz, if you cannot hold your breath for at least six months, or if you have ever wondered how you were going to pay your long-term-care insurance premium. Likewise if you do not expect the car you are currently driving to last at least fifteen more years.

If you are considering starting to collect Social Security, tell your doctor if you are taking any medications such as blood thinners, anti-depressants, mood enhancers, multi-vitamins that contain minerals, precious metals or coal tar, supplements such as St. John's Wort or ginkgo biloba, or if you regularly drink green tea, pomegranate juice or Ovaltine.

Seek immediate medical attention if your retirement presents with any combination of the following symptoms: in-grown toenails, flared nostrils, itchy palms, creaky knees, hot flashes or cold feet.

We can be certain that if retirement came with warnings and contraindications such as these, everyone would give it much more careful thought before jumping in with both feet. And then we'd probably do it anyway. After all, scary disclosures don't stop us from taking those drugs. At most, they drive us to drink. Come to think of it, that's not all bad.

# Tiger Retiree
Original Post Date Feb. 2, 2011

You may have seen some of the media coverage of the best seller written by and about the *Tiger Mom*. She's a Chinese-American who is raising her daughters using the extreme discipline favored by her own parents.

Her book has caused quite a stir, in part because the author regularly uses threats and verbal abuse to achieve her desired results. Yet not many people quibble with those results: straight-A students, star performers, acceptance to the best universities. This gave me the idea to become a Tiger Retiree—demanding the very best from my retirement and those who exert serious influence over it.

I began this quest by learning more about the Tiger Mom and what I shall delicately call her "techniques" for achieving desired outcomes. Somehow, the idea of my telling the Social Security functionary on the other end of the phone line she's "garbage" does not strike me as a way to get better results. Children are a captive audience; public servants are not.

Next I thought about how I might employ the phrase the Tiger Mom used with her daughter when she returned her daughter's handmade valentine because it wasn't up to her creative standards. I imagined myself arguing with my supplemental healthcare insurance provider over the small portion they covered on my medical claim. *"I deserve better; so I reject this"* might get the desired results for a Tiger Mom. For a Tiger Retiree, it's likely to evoke a straightforward *"Take it or leave it,"* followed by the resounding click of the phone being hung up.

Moving on to some of the Tiger Mom's axioms, I pause on: *"Nothing is fun until you're good at it."* This is how she motivates her kids to practice, practice, practice on their path to Carnegie Hall. I can think of some things in my life that became much more fun once I became good at them (and playing the piano wasn't one of them—*wink, wink.*) Still, I can't seem to come up with what I would need to do over and over related to retirement that is likely to make it more fun. Certainly not filling out claims forms, though admittedly, doing that more should make each one go more quickly. That would leave more time to do other things that actually are fun (*wink, wink* again.)

How about: *"Second is not good enough."* That seems to have some potential. It could be useful in negotiating the purchase of a condo, which I expect to be one of the first steps in our retirement. *"What! I've been outbid? Second is not good enough. What's their figure? I'll top it!"* Of course, that presumes I can afford to increase my offer—highly unlikely given what I'll probably pocket from the sale of our current house when we downsize. Still, this is one I'll mentally file away for now.

Here's one I especially like: *"Assume strength, not fragility."* The Tiger Mom is referring to what she sees as American moms' tendencies to be over-protective of their kids. Based on my recent experience having some neighbors help with our snow removal, however, I'm finding that *"assume fragility, not strength"* is a useful card for someone on the threshold of retirement to play.

By the way, over-protective parents are also referred to as "helicoptering." For me, this conjures up a different image—that of the "hovering" retiree. You've seen them. They ride around the neighborhood in a Hoveround, a souped up wheelchair that sometimes looks like a miniature mobile home. Do not confuse this with a Hovercraft; that moves on a cushion of air and requires balance and stability, neither of which most retirees have in abundance. I have no desire to become a hoverer, so I guess that means I should reject helicopter moms and by inference embrace Tiger Moms.

Still, being left with just *"Second is not good enough"* in my arsenal of Tiger Retiree techniques is not very encouraging to me. Somehow, the concept doesn't seem to be translating from motherhood to retirement. The truth is, I may have been a tiger in my salad days, but as I approach retirement, I'm really more of a pussycat.

Hmmm. Now there's a possible best-seller title: *The Pussycat Retiree*. If you have any material you think I should include, please send it on to me. I promise I won't tell you it's garbage. But I just might tell you I think you can do better. *(Wink, wink. Meow.)*

# Section IV

# What To Do
# In Retirement

# Retirement Pasttimes—Maybe You CAN Go Home Again

Original Post Date Sep. 25, 2010

One of the more pleasant aspects of retirement planning is wondering how you'll spend all that free time. Certainly I'll write more, but I look upon that as a new career, not something I'll do with my "spare" time.

Reading is one option. I never have enough time for that now. It may not be the most sensible choice for me, though. My eyes are so bad that I wear three and a quarter magnifiers around my neck at all times and keep spares in drawers throughout the house. I tire easily when I read; or more accurately, reading puts me to sleep.

Many retirees turn to volunteer work to fill their days. I'll be leaving a full-time job in the non-profit world, so volunteering isn't likely to top my list of ways to pass the time.

I could release my inner geek and renew my youthful relationship with the alto saxophone. Some of my favorite memories involve the high school band and the friends I made there. Is it realistic to take up saxophone after age 65? While many folks think I'm full of hot air, that's not the same as productive wind. Wipe those smirks off your faces.

Picture this: Me, walking around with a reed in my mouth, working to get it to the right softness so it won't squeak or split. I'm wearing a special necklace holder for my mouthpiece—the kind they give you for your glass at a wine tasting. A serious sax player always has his own mouthpiece handy, just in case he runs across a sax somewhere. I've actually had dreams about this. Maybe you really CAN go home again, but I doubt it.

It's weird enough seeing a woman my age wearing a USB jump drive on a cord around her neck. Then there's the leash with my reading glasses, and occasionally one with my driving glasses. Add another one with my sax mouthpiece, and I'll be the butt of more jokes than a bag lady. If I'm going to be known as a trendsetter, I certainly don't want it to be as the leash nerd.

That leaves the broad area of "taking up a hobby" as the most promising option for spending my free time. Over the years, I've dabbled in a variety of hobbies. Retirement will offer me the opportunity to revisit one or more of these. My shelves are filled with books on what have historically been called "distaff" arts – sewing, knitting, crocheting, needlework. It shouldn't be difficult to pick those up again, if you don't count my poor eyesight and arthritic fingers.

Turns out there are myriad TV shows on these topics. I happened to catch one when I was working from home one weekday last winter. I went into the kitchen to make some tea and turned on the TV. I distractedly clicked through the channels, curious to see what was on at that retired-people's time of day. I caught the last gasp of what appeared to be a sewing show. The hostess was what my mother would have politely called "matronly." In her best Julia Child's voice, she signed off with enormous enthusiasm: *"Thank you for joining us today to learn about stripes. Next time—checks!!"*

A fleeting vision of my post-retirement: Plopped in front of a wide screen TV. Pad and pencil at the ready to take notes on the next edition of the Julia Child of Sewing. Thinking: *"I hope I live long enough to see the show on polka dots. If there's one thing I'd regret if I were to die tomorrow, it's that I only made it through plaids."*

Shoot me now.

# Blogging—It's Tough Work

Original Post Date Sep. 29, 2010

Blogging is not easy. First you need a topic with an angle that inspires you. Then there's the writing itself. You want it to be interesting or amusing, preferably both, and you want it to flow freely in your own "voice." I started blogging to document my transition into retirement, beginning with the convoluted Medicare process. At first I posted daily, but I couldn't keep up that pace while still working.

There's a big difference between speaking and writing. People cut you more slack when you speak; you can ramble a bit, be repetitive. Writing must be net, especially for a blog. That means lots of editing. My speech can be wordy. People I worked with used to say that if you asked me what time it was, I'd tell you how a watch was made. It's now 9:18 pm, by the way. My writing is more precise because I edit ruthlessly.

When I get in the groove with a post, the process goes reasonably well. When I'm uninspired, I'd rather clean cat throw up from a wicker chair seat with an old toothbrush. Generally, I start each post by scribbling notes on a pad while I'm relaxing in our so-called family room. It's really more of a cat room. My computer is in my basement office. There's no ambient light and it's not a place of inspiration. I head there only when I'm ready to refine the scribbles.

On a recent Sunday night, after two days of jotting down posting ideas, I developed a severe pain in my right wrist. Not the kind of carpal tunnel pain that goes up your forearm and gives you tingly fingers and makes you want to eat your pillow. No, this was sharp pain caused by more of a torquing motion—the kind of motion you create when you write by hand, lying on your back with a cat on your lap. Two ibuprofen took care of the pain, but it brought home the reality that blogging would be hard work physically, too.

I may have found something to help me deal with this problem. The October 4 *Time* magazine—my source for all sorts of tidbits—has an article on power bracelets. Athletes wear them to improve their performance or to help them recuperate from injuries and maybe to screw up tests to detect steroid use. I'm interested to read that they contain holograms whose internal frequencies *"react positively to your body's natural energy field."* I suspect that one person's natural energy field is another person's bad karma—and someone else's body odor—but I read on.

The chips contain water soluble titanium that *"helps regulate the user's bioelectric body current."* That helps to improve their athletic performance, lets them recuperate faster and may increase their sexual stamina. OK. I made up that last part. This piques my curiosity. Water soluble titanium. Regulating bioelectric body current. Now we're talking real science! I'm anxious to learn how I can get my hands on one.

But wait. "Water soluble" and "electric current" in the same breath? Isn't that how people get electrocuted? Or at a very minimum, tingling fingers that are worse than the pillow-biting ones you get from carpal tunnel. I'm about to write off these bracelets as a crack pot idea and not at all suitable for my blogging torque when my eye catches something near the end of the article.

The developers are trying to get these devices into the hands of *"thought leaders"* as a way to have them go viral. You might as well have put catnip in front of a feline. Thought leader? I'm your gal! After all, the whole point of blogging is to establish oneself as someone who has ideas and opinions that other people value and want to follow mindlessly.

So, if you've been enjoying Retirement Sparks, be sure to post comments and forward the link to all your friends and relatives or, for that matter, your enemies, too. I'm going to need a lot more followers if I'm going to get my blogger's wrist into a power bracelet.

In the meantime, I'll just muddle along in excruciating pain. It's the least I can do for my people. All ten of you.

# Retirement Style—Serious vs. Lighthearted

Original Post Date Oct. 9, 2010

Retirement planning guides devote more pages to calculating how much you'll need to lead the life you desire than to how to decide what that life is. I've stumbled upon a criterion to help in that decision. What style of retirement do you want—serious or light-hearted? For example: joining an investment club—serious; playing in a band—light-hearted.

We all hope for a certain amount of balance in our retirement, but the dominant style could influence where you live, how you find new friends and what activities fill your dance card. Actually, I think those last two items may be redundant…

This came to me as I was doing email triage—read, skim, toss (or more correctly, delete). Thank you, *Time* magazine, for creating these categories in your *Briefing* section. Various criteria get my email tossed, including sender unknown, a multi-megabyte attachment, or a subject line that elicits one of those yawns so gaping it cracks your jaw hinge. It occurred to me that what separates skim from read is frequently whether it's serious or light-hearted. Simply put, I'd rather read the funny stuff than the ponderous.

Don't get me wrong. I'll ruminate as much as most folks on the important issues of our time. However, when it comes to a list of new emails that goes below the fold, I'll opt for short and funny almost every time. This was driven home to me earlier this week.

One of my college friends has lived in Canada since graduation. We keep in touch via email. She forwards all sorts of messages, from humorous lists to lengthy diatribes against the U.S. government. I can't quite figure out her political orientation—or perhaps more accurately, her husband's, as I think he's behind many of the missives. They seem to be an amalgam of Michael Moore and right wing militia.

In any event, on the same day recently, she sent an email titled *"Worth the Read"* and another *"Five Ways the Democrats Can Avoid a Catastrophe and Pull Off the Mother of All Upsets... a letter from Michael Moore."* I immediately tossed the catastrophe piece, but I opened *"Worth the Read."* It was a list of twenty or so funny thoughts, the fourth of which was *"There is great need for a sarcasm font."*

In my opinion, the need is beyond great. It could be essential to preserving society as we know it. As I read Item #4, I knew why I continue to open most of this friend's email, even though much of it fails to get past skim. It's because this friend, who early-retired quite a few years ago, still has a sense of humor. By the way, she plays in the community band, something she took up after she retired.

This led to an Oprah-like "aha!" moment. Very few of my friends seem to share my sense of humor. It wasn't always so. Am I getting crazier in my old age? Or are my friends getting stodgier?

Another college friend emailed a group of us about career networking with young alumni. I followed the embedded link to learn about the program and landed on a page with a bar chart showing how many alumni in each decade participate. Our graduation decade, the sixties, wasn't there. I replied-to-all that they must not be interested in old farts like us.

My expectation was to evoke similarly sarcastic comments. Perhaps: *"Oh we're there, but our numbers are so small, we're just a flat line, not a bar."* I received two replies. One explained how important seniors are to the program, since we have valuable experience and we're reaching a stage where we also have time to devote. The other was similarly serious. Looking back, I wish I'd had that sarcasm font for my comment.

I wonder what implications this has for my retirement. If I relocate where people are very serious, will I feel out of place? Will I have trouble making new friends? Or can I find folks with a sense of humor if I choose the right activities? Let me think a minute. If you've read my earlier posts, you know about my high school days as a band geek. My sister, who lives in Vermont where we'll be moving, belongs to an investment club.

Perhaps her club would invest in a used saxophone so I can join the community band. *(Insert sarcasm font here.)*

# Retirement Projects—Experiments for Idle Hands

Original Post Date Nov. 20, 2010

Like many folks, I've been contemplating how I'll occupy myself after I retire—besides writing more. What sort of projects will fill my days of leisure? I think I've found the answer. I'm going to conduct freelance science experiments.

A recent *New York Times* article reported on research into the question *"How do cats drink?"* It was prompted by the observation that cats drink far more neatly than dogs. I'm a long-time cat lover and owner, but I have not been kept up nights wondering about this. Apparently, a group of engineers has.

Four of them collaborated on experiments to probe this issue. These were no backwater engineers; they work at MIT, VPI and Princeton—or did anyway. Who knows how their institutions will react to their report in *Science* on cat-lapping.

The team concluded that cats lap by balancing *"opposing gravitational and inertial forces."* The tip of the cat's tongue touches the water surface. Then they pull it up quickly, *"drawing a column of water behind it."* There was a lot more information, such as lapping frequency for optimal efficiency relative to the cat's size, and so on. It was very much the type of data one would expect to see in *Science*.

The *Times* article implied that the research was conducted on the scientist's own time, but we all know what that means. What was clearly stated is that the project required no financing; the robot used in the experiment was *"borrowed... from a neighboring lab."*

Although I doubt I have neighbors from whom I can borrow robots for my retirement projects, I feel confident I can devise experiments that employ ordinary household materials. The trick will be to find issues to probe that have been overlooked by scientists, but are of burning interest to ordinary people. People who might read my blog.

Here's one example. Cat owners know there is an irresistible magnetic force between cat hair and their owner's clothes. We also know that the strength of that attraction increases the more disparate the tone of the cat's fur and the owner's attire. A white cat will shed far more hair onto its owner's black lap than onto her white sweater.

I shall devise an experiment to determine why this happens. I fully expect static electricity to play a role in my research. I'll also measure whether or not the attraction of black hair to white clothing is equal to its inverse. I can see some of you black-cat owners out there nodding *"It most definitely is."* When I'm done, there will be scientific proof and we'll know for certain.

There may be skeptics among you thinking: *"She won't be able to answer questions like these without a fancy laboratory."* Consider the following account that my nephew shared many years ago. It was one of the winning entries in some contest similar to the Darwin Awards, but for clever inventions.

We know that cats always land on their feet when they fall—or are dropped—from heights. Murphy's Law also tells us that a piece of buttered toast will always land buttered-side down. The budding inventor who won the competition combined these two pieces of information to devise a perpetual motion machine. Here's how you build it.

Strap a row of well-buttered toast along the back of large cat. Drop the cat from a substantial height. As it starts to fall, the cat will turn paw-side down so it can land on its feet. The toast will counter by flipping the cat's back toward the floor, so the toast can land buttered-side down. These two opposing forces will set the cat into a spin that will keep it airborne indefinitely, thus creating a perpetual motion machine.

I rest my case.

# Creative Sparks

Original Post Date Dec. 4, 2010

When I hear about reunions with people I haven't been in touch with for thirty or forty years, I don't rush to put them on my calendar in ink. Until recently, with the exception of my fellow band geeks, I hadn't given much thought to what my high school classmates might have done with their lives. Ditto for my summer crowd

It was a 45 minute bus ride to my regional high school, where only 40 per cent of the students went on to college. The cute guys were more likely to be in auto mechanics and shop than in my calculus or physics classes. Let me amend that. The bad boys that I found fascinating were more likely to be mechanics and shoppies.

We lived year round in a summer community, and the seasonal folks came from all around our state. Looking back, it makes sense that they had the potential to become really interesting adults. But adult potential wasn't something that concerned me.

Here is my deep dark secret. I was a shallow teenager, not prone to introspection and philosophizing. I was more interested in how attractive my girlfriend's brother had become during his freshman year in college. Or the muscles that my brother's beach buddies had developed over the winter.

One thing that has surprised me about the people from my past with whom I've reconnected as I approach retirement is how interesting they seem to be. They are smart and well-traveled—one was even in the Peace Corps. The biggest revelation is that they are amazingly creative, especially those who are already retired. This gives me hope for my own retirement.

One of my summer friends does puppetry with her husband. She studied it in Prague decades ago. We're talking serious stuff, not faces drawn on your fingertips in ball point pen. A college classmate took up clarinet late in life and is totally immersed in her community band. My brother, who retired very early, became a fabulous outdoor photographer once he had the time to pursue it.

I used to do all sorts of artsy things. The company where I worked had a holiday doll pageant. They provided naked dolls—no snickering, please—and asked employees to make or buy outfits for them so they could be donated. They gave prizes in four categories for the handmade outfits. I won first prize thirteen years in a row and eventually captured first in each of the four categories. Mutter *"competitive b- - -h"* all you want, but I truly enjoyed doing it.

Perhaps retirement will afford me the time and the opportunity to take up new artistic pursuits, like photography. I bought a Nikon digital camera several years ago, but my eyes are so bad, I have trouble focusing. Jagdish would like to learn ballroom dancing. He has two left feet and I've broken both of mine—mercifully, not at the same time. Also, his rhythm is distinctly Indian, and then there's my diminishing sense of balance. Dancing doesn't seem too promising an option. I suppose writing is creative, but I was hoping for something more… well, artsy. Or flamboyant?

I'm sitting here, trying to feel creative, looking around for inspiration. My computer keyboard catches my eye. Some of the keys are almost completely clean, while others have dark, smudgy spots around their perimeters. I wonder why all the keys aren't smudged. The cleanest ones are the home row, and the dirtiest are the numbers. Maybe Lily walks along the upper edge with her dirty paws and the keys I use most often are the cleanest. But the function keys on the very top row are also clean. There goes the Lily theory. I'm perplexed. I'm also tempted to go get some Q-tips and cleaning fluid.

Then I get into Jagdish's glass half empty/half full mode of thought. (See "A Shifting Line in the Sand" in "Retirement Planning.") Were the keys with the white spots in the middle at one point totally smudged, so now are half clean? Or were the white spots never covered, and somehow the smudges only accumulated around the perimeter, so now half dirty?

It doesn't say much for my creative sparking that I'm so easily distracted by a computer keyboard. I'm feeling quite inadequate compared to my peers. What we have here is a failure to find a muse. I don't know about you, but if there's one place I'd expect to find my muse, it's at the bottom of a—you guessed it—lovely bottle of *vino*.

See ya!

# Just Open the Darn Book!

Original Post Date Dec. 11, 2010

A friend of mine who is about nine months ahead of me on the retirement timeline has been trying to decide when to stop working. He can afford to do it now, but as he told one of his colleagues, he doesn't know yet what he wants to do with the next phase of his life. He lost his wife about two years ago, so his long-held plans have changed.

His feeling was, if he didn't have a plan, why not keep working? The advice his colleague* gave him was simple, yet profound. He said: *"You can't start writing the next chapter of your life unless you're willing to open the book."* I decided it would be a good idea to think about some of the headings on the pages of my life's next chapter.

The first one is easy: Give away all the alarm clocks in the house and sleep in every morning. That would require some planning, though, because Lily would be walking all over me at some point, wanting her breakfast. I started a list: "Things to Buy for Next Chapter of My Life." Then I wrote "gravity-feed cat food dispenser."

Another page should be: Read all the books that I bought and never had time to finish. Or even start. Of course, most of those books will have been sold or donated by the time we downsize for retirement. I add to the list: "Buy a Kindle." Or whatever electronic reading device *du jour* makes sense for a Mac lover. And then "Find out if Kindle comes with 3.25 magnifier." I amend that to "Find out maximum Kindle magnifier number" and "Auto upgrades available?" By next year, I might be up to 3.5.

I title a page: Take up scrap-booking, or making greeting cards. I have lots of supplies that I've collected over the years. Somehow that sounds too crafty, not artsy enough for me. Maybe collage. Or book making. No, not the taking bets kind. The type where you bind your own books with handmade paper; it's quite popular now. Although setting myself up as a bookie could be a way to supplement my retirement income. Hmmm…

Definitely: Start a vegetable and herb garden. Note to self: Do not plant anything in the catnip family—that means no mint. I tried growing catnip once, and the neighbor's cat—an outdoor scamp—mowed it to ground level. He got so drunk that he trashed the entire herb bed. My own cats never saw so much as a leaf off the *nepeta cataria*.

This reminds me of how my father planted various fruit trees on our modest sized property in New Jersey. My favorite was the Carpathian walnut tree. I am not joking. My mother baked a lot of tea breads as gifts and many of them contained walnuts. Since those were pricey, my father decided to save money by planting the tree. He did not take into account the local squirrel population. Despite various attempts at curtailing their thievery—an entire post in itself, he was never able to harvest enough for more than one batch of bread. He eventually chopped down the walnut tree out of spite.

Perhaps: Volunteer at the Best Friends animal sanctuary in Utah. My friend, Sheryl, named them to receive contributions when she died. Their work is amazing and the DVDs they send tug at your heartstrings even more than that *"Arms of an Angel"* SPCA commercial. You know, the three-tissue anti-cruelty one with the dogs in cages and the Sarah McLachlan song in the background. If I went to Best Friends, I might never come back. Besides, I doubt I could bring Lily and Luke, and I can't really picture Jagdish mucking horse stalls…

Suddenly I'm inspired. I have the perfect heading for the next chapter of my life. Become a boutique wine maker. It brings together so many aspects of the other ideas. I can save money. I'll have gifts to give. I'll be a classic Virgo, working with the earth. And we all know what the best part of making my own wine will be. *Santé!*

*Credit to Michael Fine, even though he doesn't know it.

# Marking How Time Passes
Original Post Date Dec. 18, 2010

As someone who is still fully employed, I tend to mark the passage of time by certain repetitive tasks in the office. If I'm making a bank deposit, another week has passed. When I'm submitting the payroll, two weeks have gone by, and so on. I use the calendar on my computer to remind me of various things, including what day of the week it is.

Recently I received a robo-call that one of my prescriptions on auto-refill was ready for pick-up. My first thought was: *"Has a month gone by already?"* Then it occurred to me. Once I'm retired, those robo-calls could be the only way I'll know another month has passed.

Will I realize another week is history only when Lily starts looking askance at the litter boxes because they need changing? Gray roots of my hair crying out to be colored? Four weeks gone, but I'll probably put it off another week. If I'm not working, I can go as gray as Jamie Lee Curtis. But not if that means I have to start eating Activia.

It seems there will be reliable ways to have a sense of the passage of time from one week upward. But what about knowing which day of the week it is when I wake up each morning?

Most of us have had the Monday Morning Blues at some point in our working lives and we're all familiar with TGIF. There's no reason for Monday blues when you can sleep in every day. No, I'll need to find a new way to figure out what day it is.

Perhaps I'll get some useful direction from that old nursery rhyme about Monday being wash day, Tuesday ironing, etc. By the way, it never made sense to me that mending day followed washing and ironing. Shouldn't you mend things before you wash them, so the holes don't get bigger as the agitator… well, agitates? And surely ironing and then mending is a recipe for re-ironing. Well, it is if you've ever seen me mend anything.

A Google search shows that in its original version this rhyme had Thursday as churning day and Friday as cleaning. More recent ones dropped churning (has no one heard of metaphors?), bumped up cleaning a day, and slipped in shopping on Friday. I have no quibble with getting a day to shop. Just saying, in this complex world, our houses probably "churn" even more than that little one on the prairie did.

While the specifics of the rhyme weren't of much use, the concept helped me. Herewith my plan for how Jagdish and I will mark time passing once we've retired.

*Sunday will be puzzle day—Sudoku, Times and such.*
*The polit shows will fill the morn, so we're not out of*
*touch.*

*Monday's tagged for exercise; perhaps we'll walk a bit.*
*Unless Jagdish's knees give out, in which case we'll just*
*sit.*

*Tuesday it's the Internet, I'll write and chase my dream.*
*Jagdish will also be there with some money-making*
*scheme.*

*Wednesday on to household chores, each week a differ-*
*ent one.*
*We'll wash and clean and press and mend from dawn to*
*setting sun. [As if.]*

*Thursday can be artsy time, pursuing crafty fads.*
*With glue sticks, fabric scraps and some recycled paper*
*bags.*

*Friday we will grocery shop and cook and bake things*
*fine.*
*And then we'll settle back to sip a lovely glass of wine.*
*[Or two. Or three.]*

*Saturday's for scouring every type of publication.*
*It's how I'll get ideas to free up scriber's constipation.*
*[Writer's block?]*

*So there you have the weekly plan of how our days will*
*pass.*
*And every night I'll find some time to raise that long-*
*stemmed glass.*

# Things I Won't Be Doing

Original Post Date Jan. 19, 2011

My original plans had me retiring at the end of last year. Yesterday, I drove to work during a winter storm and drove home in flooding rains, thinking: *"This is exactly what I was looking forward to NOT doing once I retired."* That of course had me thinking more broadly that retirement planning involves not just deciding what I want to do when I stop working full time, but also what I don't want to do.

Top on the list is that I don't want to have to get out of bed on mornings when winter storms are raging and the walk is no longer visible and the cars need scraping. I want to grab the nearest cat and cuddle. I don't want to worry about whether I'll be able to dig out in time to make an 8:30 AM meeting.

I don't want to have to make the next day's lunches the night before, especially when I'm really tired. I don't want to feel guilty when we open the refrigerator in the morning, lunch totes in hand, and discover I never made sandwiches the night before.

I also do not want to do my grocery shopping on the weekends, when everyone else is in the market and the only cart I can find has at least one wheel that refuses to roll. Or it has a large plastic automobile mounted on the front, waiting for a toddler to drive it.

It would be nice to be able to forget about wearing pantyhose except on occasions when I'll be doing something I really want to dress up for. Which means not very often, I suspect. Yes, I'll keep a few of my business suits with the pencil skirts, just in case, but only because of Murphy's law.

I don't want to say "no" to joining committees and going to events that interest me but I don't have time for and "yes" to ones I don't care about, but are politically correct for my job.

I don't want to have to tell my friends that I can't have dinner with them next Wednesday night even though my calendar is free, because I have a full schedule on Thursday, so I'll need to get to bed early.

I don't want to have to spend Sunday night dying my roots when the gray is just slightly visible but I have a meeting the next week where I don't want to look my age. The gray needs coloring soon enough without pushing the schedule. Now that I think about it, I don't want to have to attend any meetings where I care if I look my age.

Simply put: I want to be a spoiled, rotten, petulant adult. I don't want to have to do anything unless I choose to do it. So there.

# Seeking Identity
Original Post Date Mar. 19, 2011

This morning I woke up and realized that I'm finally retired. I am no longer the Executive Director of a nonprofit federation. On my "to do" list: get new business cards, but I won't be running off to Staples to get ones that read "Elaine M. Decker, Retiree." Also unacceptable is: "Executive Director, *Emerita*;" it puts the focus on what I was, not what I am. It looks like I need to find a new identity.

Obviously, I'm a blogger. Some of you know I'm also a freelance writer. Combining those gives several choices. "Frogger" is the most obvious, and while I admit to being a Francophile, "frogger" sounds too condescending. It also reminds me of the nickname my brother's dorm mates gave him when they learned his hometown was Green Pond.

"Flogger" is no improvement, as it implies that I beat my writing into submission. True, I edit a lot, and "wordsmith" may be a cousin to "blacksmith," but I do not beat my words. Nor do I mince them. Slice them and dice them, perhaps. Massage them, certainly. But flog them? Never.

Then there is "freeger," which sounds like some nefarious trade or a delivery method for illicit drugs. Switching the order of things gives me "bleeger," which too closely resembles the surname of a tousle-haired young singer with first name Justin.

"Bloglancer" feels too archaic for my edgy writing, while "bliter" makes it sound like my writing disfigures the literary landscape. No need to weigh in on that one, thank you.

Some other hats I wear are marketer and web developer. That gives us "webmarker" and "marloper," both of which leave me cold. Although I could live with "marvel," it's not a good fit with my self-deprecating tone.

Clearly the concatenation approach is not bearing usable fruit. I need to think more esoterically. I'm a philosopher—too stuffy—and a ruminator—conjuring up images that remind me that a post-retirement goal is to exercise more. Not something I'd want on my business cards.

"Satirist" is a possibility, given my style, but I'd worry people would think "satyress," considering how often wine shows up in my posts. "Entrepreneur" is another option, especially if it brings good karma so I make some money from my various ventures. Of course, we all know how likely that is.

As a last resort, I could always append a status word to the end of my name. Several of my attorney friends have cards that read: Legal Eagle, Esquire. Since I probe the pressing issues of our day, perhaps mine could read: Elaine M. Decker, Inquire—too much like a newspaper. Or, looking to my desire to become the female Dave Barry: Elaine M. Decker, Aspire—too... well, aspirational.

It looks like this is going to take some time to sort out. But I should probably make it a point to do it soon. The last thing I want is to have my cards read: Elaine M. Decker, Expired. It would give ironic new meaning to having the last word.

# Retirement Vacations—Places We Remember

Original Post Date Apr. 6, 2011

Retirees have plenty of time to go on the vacations they've always planned on. Unfortunately, they don't always have plenty of money to pay for them. As a service to my fellow retirees on fixed incomes, I've researched a variety of affordable vacation packages. These are sure to provide memories you will treasure.

## California Botanical Delights

Travel to California to go to the San Francisco Flower Show. To get into the spirit of things, be sure to wear some flowers in your hair. Stop by the thrilling Fruit Exposition up on Blueberry Hill in nearby San José (if you know the way...). We recommend the optional side excursion to Napa wine country, where the air is fresher, the kisses are sweeter and the Pinot is always ready for a summer of love.

## Buffet Lovers Getaway

For those who love the salt air and yards-long tables of food, but are on low-sodium diets, the popular Buffet Lovers Key West package is the perfect weekend getaway. Spend four days and three nights in Margaritaville. Extras include: guided tour of sponge cake factory reputedly owned by Jimmy Buffet, discount on tattoo by island artist Mexican Cutie, and all the frozen concoctions you can drink. Best of all, you won't have to worry about any lost shaker of salt. Package includes plenty of low-sodium sea salt for your meals—or wherever you want to use it.

## Glen Campbell Memorial Circuit

The special Glen Campbell Memorial Circuit celebrates the cities he immortalized in his chart-topping songs. Trip kicks off in Phoenix, and by the time you get there, the world's oldest, star spangled rodeo in nearby Prescott will be in full swing. Then it's on to Kansas, where you'll be a guest at an exclusive meet-and-greet with the original Wichita Cable Guy. Final stop: Galveston, where you can hear those sea waves crashing and look out beyond the sea. Oh, wait. That was Bobby Darin… You'll also get a souvenir BeDazzler gem setter so you can come home looking like a Rhinestone Cowboy.

## Rock and Roll Nostalgia Tour

Rock around the clock on a unique, nostalgic trip to Memphis. It starts with a visit to Graceland, but the real jewel is a private tour of the Rock and Roll Clothing Museum. You begin in the prom room, where you'll see Marty Robbins' white sport coat with a pink carnation—freeze dried (the carnation, not Robbins) and Elvis's blue suede shoes. Also there—prom dresses in blue velvet and Chantilly lace. Special footwear collection includes white bucks, saddle shoes and bobby sox, and of course, tan shoes with pink shoe laces. For an extra fee, get photographed in the original teeny weenie, yellow polka dot bikini or Dooley's polka dot vest and big panama with a purple hatband. Museum reproductions of all items are available in the gift shop, and seniors get a 5% discount.

## Magical Islands Cruise

This is the perfect autumn vacation for those who enjoy the wind and the mist in their hair. Cruise the Hawaiian Islands on a boat with billowed sails. Ports of call include Kailua-Kona, Waikiki, and finally, on the island of Kauai, Poipu Beach and the mystical land of Honalee. Known for its magical potions and puffs of gentle breezes, Honalee is guaranteed to bring enchanted memories. String and sealing wax come with the package.

All tours include local ground transportation. Taxes are extra. Space is limited, so sign up early to be assured to get the tour of your choice.

I'm seriously considering the Napa excursion—surprise, surprise. On the other hand, I've always secretly wanted to get a tattoo. Well, not on the other hand, actually…

# The Fine Art of Napping

Original Post Date Sep. 3, 2011

One of the great joys of retirement is being able to take a nap whenever I want. One of the downsides is that I seem to want to nap a lot. I've made an in-depth study of the subject and I've identified ten variations of the nap.

The most familiar is the opportunistic catnap, so named because cats have perfected this midday snooze. The best thing about this type is that you can take one anywhere. However, my considerable research shows that the best place is stretched out on your back, usually on a couch, with the sun on your face. If you're not sure if the nap you are taking is this type, check your midsection when you wake up. If there's a cat on top of you, you've just enjoyed a catnap.

Another type many of you will recognize is the post-prandial nap. This one occurs after a big meal, especially a holiday dinner. Men are particularly fond of post-prandials, except when there's football on TV. My research shows that retirees become increasingly prone to these naps midafternoon, especially after a larger-than-usual lunch. Post-prandials are most appropriately taken in an overstuffed chair. They're often short, yet highly effective.

The alcohol-induced nap is related to the post-prandial, but has its own profile. For one thing, you don't need to have eaten before taking this type. It's most commonly seen after wine tastings, including the ones you have alone in your own home. Many of my most enjoyable naps have occurred during what some might call a "wine stupor." I prefer to think of them as research projects. The duration of this type depends on how much alcohol you've consumed and whether you've collapsed onto something comfortable.

Another nap familiar to retirees is the reading-induced one. This is characterized by the body positioned in a comfortable chair, reading material in hand. You may not realize you've had this nap until you wake up and find your reading glasses on your lap and your book on the floor. The older I get, the fewer pages it takes to induce a reading nap.

A variation on this nap is the TV-induced nod off. Body position is generally the same a for the reading one. Political speeches are especially effective at luring me into this type. It doesn't matter which party is speaking. These days I'll nod off for the President just as easily as for a Tea Party rebuttal.

Likewise, the older I get the more often I need an exercise recovery nap, which is most effective when you're splayed out on a pile carpet. Mowing the lawn takes 45 minutes, including emptying the clippings into an approved brown paper sack. You know, the ones you buy at Home Depot.

They come up to my armpits, so I have to lift the clippings catcher to head height to empty it. I find this more exhausting than the mowing itself. By the time I'm done, I'm ready for a snooze.

A related type, the battery-recharger, replenishes emotional or psychic energy. For example: the robocall for my pharmacy's auto-refill doesn't work with one of my prescriptions. It's taken weekly on an empty stomach, with a half-hour wait after. If I run out, it messes up my Sunday. I spent an hour on this with a customer service rep who had what I'll charitably describe as a lack of understanding of the situation. By the time I hung up, I was badly in need of a nap to recharge my psychic battery.

The boredom nap sneaks up on you when you have nothing exciting planned for the day, but you're not really sure you care. You stretch out someplace comfortable to contemplate some possibilities, and the next thing you know… ZZZZZ.

Rainy day naps are one of the great guilty pleasures of retirees. The flexibility of our schedules allows us to curl up somewhere cozy, soft and warm when the weather's bad. Maybe we'll grab some reading material; maybe we'll grab a cat to cuddle. More likely we'll grab an afghan that's been in the family for decades and just sink in for a comfortable snooze. Eat your hearts out, those of you still working.

Lastly, the procrastinator nap is best taken when you have a long list of projects that need attention, but you just don't want to tackle any of them. This type is another guilty pleasure of retirees. We can procrastinate as much as we want without risk of serious repercussions. Except, of course, if the task at hand is writing one's weekly blog post.

Not to worry. As long as I've had my quota of catnaps, postprandials and battery-rechargers, I'm not likely to be lured by the procrastinator. I'm far more likely to miss a posting date because I've succumbed to an alcohol-induced nap. Now that this post is ready to go, I think I'll pour myself a nice glass of *vino* and see where it takes me.

# Section V

# General Observations
# On Retirement

# What If There Were a Final Exam?
Original Post Date Oct. 2, 2010

Last night I had one of those anxiety-laden dreams that most of us have now and then. It was the one where you're late for a final exam and you forgot to study.

For me, those dreams usually follow a dinner of marbleized red meat or highly-spiced food. The rotisserie chicken I had last night was supposed to be the plain version. It dreamed more like lemon pepper coated with Tex-Mex and it just wouldn't go away. Finally I got out of bed to re-brush and floss and drink more water. My hope was to banish any last remnant of the meal, and the dream along with it.

When I got back into bed, the dream mutated into a nightmare. Now I was stressed over a final exam to qualify for retirement. The scariest part was that it seemed perfectly reasonable that the government could require such a test.

*Question 1: What is your full retirement age?* That's easy: 66. A bell sounds. This is going to be a piece of cake.

*Next question: Part I. How much money can you earn after retirement before Uncle Sam starts taxing your Social Security benefit? Part II. Does that figure include your Social*

*Security money or is it in addition to it?* I have no idea. That's why I have an accountant handle my taxes. I take a guess at $25,000. A buzzer sounds.

*Question 3: When did Social Security begin and what was the original name of the act?* I decide to Google this one so I don't get it wrong. (It's comforting to know we can Google in our dreams.) I learn that it started in 1935 and it was originally named the Economic Security Act. This strikes me as so hilarious that I hardly hear the bell through my peals of laughter. Economic security. Talk about an oxymoron.

*Question 4: What percentage of people die within two years of starting to collect their Social Security?* Government test preparers have a warped sense of humor. I Google. I Bing. I Ask Jeeves. No one can tell me this. I have the uneasy feeling it's a larger percentage than I want to know, so I say a comfortingly low 5% and wait for the buzzer.

*Question 5: Name the three rock-and-roll icons killed in a plane crash in 1959.* I know this one. I start writing: Buddy Holly, The Big Bopper, and Richie Valens. I'm surprised to hear the buzzer again. Turns out I've spelled Ritchie's first name wrong. As a side note, this reminds me that I still have a box of LP's and some 45's to get rid of.

Clearly this test is targeted to those on the cusp of the baby boom. I wonder if they're trying to stress us into heart failure so we won't be around to collect Social Security. I also start to wonder how many questions I can get wrong and still pass.

*Question 6: What actress played Lara's grown daughter (aka "the girl") in Doctor Zhivago?* Are you kidding me? How does that movie relate to retirement in the US? It happens that I was obsessed with *Dr. Zhivago*, so I know it was Rita Tushingham. In my dream, I see her clearly, carrying the balalaika. As the bell rings, I drift into visions of Julie Christie in a snowy wonderland. She's wearing a fur bonnet, tied under her chin. It's the same as the one my parents surprised me with at Christmas the year the movie came out.

I remember that I still have that hat in a box in the cedar closet up on the third floor. It's not something I'll need when I retire, so I make a mental note to add it to the donation pile in the morning.

Suddenly my dream is filled with ringing bells, like the stock exchange has erupted. A sign pops up: *You've passed your retirement test.*

I guess these questions had a purpose after all. When I woke up, I had a feeling of accomplishment. Not only had I passed my test, but I also had several cartons of stuff mentally earmarked to lighten the load when we downsize. Not a bad haul for a night of crazy dreams, but I think I'll lay off the rotisserie chicken for awhile.

# The Arc of Life—Bell Curve Or Swoosh?

Original Post Date Oct. 27, 2010

Picking up on Saturday's post: I thought things would get simpler as I approach retirement. Instead they are more complicated. I expected the arc of my life to be a bell curve, with the X axis for complexity and the Y for the years. Life would start out very simple, get progressively more complicated, and gradually get simpler once again toward the end. I'm finding it more of a Nike-like swoosh, trending upward in its complexity.

The possibility that life will keep getting increasingly complicated is scary. If I remember my physics classes, to get a bell curve, I'd need to find external forces to exert pressure on the end of that swoosh to bend it down into one of Malcolm Gladwell's long tails. There's something inherently contradictory in it being so complicated to get simpler. With my luck, the swoosh would coil in on itself, creating a spring. I have a vision of me being flung off into space, where I'll drift for eternity among the other debris in the upper atmosphere. So much for a long tail and metaphors.

It gets me thinking about graphing other aspects of life going into retirement. The Y axis will always be years, but the X can be so many other things. Here's how I see some of them.

Income is generally a bell curve, while expenses are usually a bell curve ending in a swoosh of medical expenses. Of course, if one becomes a successful author later in life, income could be a swoosh, too. (Once again a shameless appeal for more of you to follow my blog.)

Number of friends – sadly, a bell curve. However, friends to whom you are connected can be a swoosh, thanks to Facebook. As a matter of fact, a recent AARP survey of 3,000 plus people 45 and up shows that loneliness decreases after age 60. They probably conducted the survey in those retire-ment communities in Florida where they specialize in line dances and member-produced Gilbert & Sullivan operettas.

Moving on. The hair on your head – bell curve (women included). Original teeth in your mouth – bell curve. The food you can eat – bell curve. Babies start out with limited diets and lots of soft mushy food. Need I say more?

My husband's weight – bell curve; my weight – *swoo-oo-oosh!* I've often said there should be a law against husbands weighing less than their wives. Unfortunately, Jagdish won't put on even a pound or two of sympathy weight. Ailments, aches and pains, medications – *swoosh, swoosh, swoosh.*

Sex – generally a bell curve, although some retirees claim it's a major swoosh. Not that I want to give too much away about my life in the sixties and seventies, but those retirees must have had pretty tame sex in their salad days if senior sex is considered swooshy.

I could go on for several more pages, but you get the idea. Feel free to weigh in with suggestions of your own. As I re-read this posting, I'm sensing a pattern here. The things that you would like to be a bell curve are generally a swoosh. The things you'd welcome as a swoosh are bell curves. It's as though some higher power is playing a cruel mathematical game with us as we grow older—a game that goes on until we flat line.

I decide to make "A Grand Plan" for when I retire. I'm going to focus on one curve each year to see if I can change its aspect to something more favorable. Maybe I'll start with turning sex into a swoosh again. That should make my husband happy. I hope I don't get too caught up in this metaphor. Another vision of me, this time whispering sweet nothings in Jagdish's ear. As I see that swoosh taking shape, I reflexively shout Nike's tag line: *"Just do it!"*

That sound you hear is our sex curve flat lining.

# Species of Retirees

Original Post Date Dec. 22, 2010

The end of the year always sees the publication of various lists. *Time*'s end-December 2010 issue featured a list of ten new species, including the Tube-Nosed Fruit Bat, the Bluetooth Tarantula and the Giant Woolly Rat. I do not lie.

As I've collected information for my retirement, I've identified a number of distinct species of retirees. One of the most familiar is the Pot-Bellied Pensioner. He was fortunate to spend his entire working life at one large corporation. They gave him an irresistible buyout that has enabled him to sit back and do nothing at all. His lack of motivation to augment his discretionary income has resulted in a substantial weight gain around his midsection, which has led to considerable health problems. He doesn't care, however, because his package included full health care coverage. The good news is that this species of retiree is on the verge of extinction.

A large but relatively young group are the Double-Dipping Unionites. These former government functionaries and public servants received lucrative retirement packages around age 40, at which time they took a second job. That job provided a similarly lucrative package that kicked in around age 60. Although I don't have sufficient data to prove my theory, I believe there's an unwritten but clearly understood system of job swapping among the Double Dippers. At age 40, those in career A trade places with those in career B, so at age 60, they all retire with double dips. If enough of our cities and states go bankrupt, thus voiding existing contracts, this species may one day become extinct, too. Don't hold your breath.

Those of you who live in the more progressive states have surely seen the Downy-Chested Community Organizer. Dressed in a pouffy insulated vest in winter, this activist retiree goes door to door trying to drum up enthusiasm, signatures and contributions. She champions such causes as Save the Bay, Don't Feed the Pigeons, Protect the Tube-Nosed Fruit Bat and Free the Giant Woolly Rats. This type of retiree shows no signs of impending extinction.

A particularly flamboyant species I identified is the Condo Commodore. Often self-appointed, but sometimes elected to his position, he patrols your community looking for violations of condo rules. Weather permitting, he's dressed in a navy blazer with brass buttons, khaki slacks and white patent leather loafers. If he's a widower you're done for. The widows in the community will never support an uprising against him.

Most of you will recognize the Peripatetic Busy Bee. She worries about being marginalized by her circle of friends who are still working. So she packs her calendar so chock-a-block full of meetings, event and trips, that is seems like she suffers from adult-onset ADHD. Call her for an impromptu get together and she'll tell you she can't possibly meet you for at least a month. And by the way, if you're in her neighborhood over the next two weeks, would you please water her plants? She'll be away in Tanzania with her African Violet Club.

An unfortunately common species is the Red-Nosed Walmart Greeter. Most of us are familiar with the three-legged stool concept of funding one's retirement (Social Security, some sort of income from a former employer, and your own 401K/IRA type of investment program.) Sadly, the Red-Nosed Walmart Greeter has a one-legged stool—the wobbly one of Social Security. She balances precariously on that stool at the door of your local Walmart, alternately smiling a greeting and dabbing at her leaky nose with the corner of her blue pinny. It seems as though the vital fluids of her life are draining slowly out of her, but it's probably just hay fever.

The most obnoxious retiree is the Smug-Mouthed Investment Wizard. This migratory creature had the foresight (and the time) to carefully manage his investments from age 40 onward. He and his spouse bought real estate at the low points in the market and sold at the high. They now own retirement-appropriate homes in every climate that the calendar requires, and they make sure everyone knows when they're making their winter pilgrimage to Sanibel Island. On the brighter side, each time they return to the north country, their skin looks more and more like leather. There is a god after all.

# Signs It's Time to Retire

Original Post Date Jan. 29, 2011

This week it hit home for me that if you pay attention, you'll see clear signals when it's time to retire. Here are some that I've uncovered.

*You know it's time to retire when:*
You come home from work following an afternoon snowstorm to find that one of your neighbors shoveled your drive and your walk without your even having to ask. [OMG! We're now that elderly couple in the neighborhood that everyone feels sorry for.]

*You know it's time to retire when:*
The store manager who never offered to carry your 20-pound bag of cat litter to the car wants to know if you need help with a box of Clementines.

*You know it's time to retire when:*
The same alarm clock that used to jolt you out of bed the second it went off can no longer rouse you from your sleep enough to provoke you to hit the snooze button. [Maybe it was the wine…]

*You know it's time to retire when:*

You look forward to spending some time doing a few loads of laundry and you feel like you've won the lottery when all the socks match.

*You know it's time to retire when:*

You get excited at the prospect of shredding a stack of paperwork, especially ten-year-old tax returns. [And older.]

*You know it's time to retire when:*

Two out of three messages on your answering machine are prescription pick-up reminders for you or your spouse. [Don't you just love that auto-refill service?]

*You know it's time to retire when:*

Your computer calendar has more doctors' appointments on it than business meetings. [Like mine next week.]

And finally—

*You know it's time to retire when:*

The progression of what you wear in winter goes (for women) from just a bra under your top, to an undershirt over your bra, to just an undershirt. ["Perky" has lost its appeal, especially in cold weather.] And (for men) from a dress shirt and tie to a sweater vest over a sport shirt to a plaid flannel shirt over thermal underwear.

If you recognize three of more of these signs in your own life, you should be a regular follower of *RetirementSparks*, because your own retirement can't be far over the horizon. I've seen all the signs, so I shall lead the way into that mysterious black rabbit hole. If you don't keep hearing from me via regular blog posts, send reinforcements.

On second thought, send chocolate. And wine, of course.

# Neighborhood Security Alerts
Original Post Date Feb. 5, 2011

The Homeland Security Advisory System of color-coded terrorism alerts will be replaced in a few months. The old system had five levels, the highest being red (severe). Many of you don't know what the lowest colors are, since we've been on a constant level three (yellow, or elevated) or occasionally higher ever since the system was put in place. [The bottom levels are green (low) and blue (guarded), BTW.]

We're promised that the new "formal" alerts will be issued only when there is a specific threat, that they'll include steps authorities are taking and what the public can do, and that they'll have a specified end date. Can't wait.

No really, I don't think we can wait for this new system to take shape and for all the bugs and hiccups to be shaken out. We need a new system right now and I have it all figured out. My system is designed specifically for residential neighborhoods—retirement communities in particular. It's based on the neighborhood watch programs that are already in place to deter crime, but it's more nuanced.

Like the original Homeland Security Advisory System, my Neighborhood Security Alerts have five levels. The first is

*Be Aware*, and the street sign for this is a pair of eyes peering out from the darkness. When you see those eyes posted, keep your own wide open, looking for suspicious behavior in your neighborhood. At this threat level, simply letting the perpetrators know you're on to them should be enough to stifle them.

The second level is *Be Alert*. Its sign has a pair of ears, spread out like funnels to catch the slightest noise that's out of the ordinary. This sign tells you to tune in to every conversation in every neighbor's yard. For best results, get a compact recording device and hold it in prominent view. That should serve as a deterrent to anyone plotting to overthrow those in power. Even if not, it will help you provide useful testimony in court, just before you enter the witness protection program.

Level three is *Watch Closely*, with a pair of binoculars on the signage. When you see this, go out of your way to inspect your neighbors' yards and look through their curtainless windows in search of questionable activity. Don't be shy about it. As a member of the Neighborhood Security Alert team, you are empowered to engage in all sorts of despicable behavior. Don't waste that opportunity. You'd be surprised what goes on behind those closed doors. Or maybe you wouldn't be...

Next—and the second highest level—is *Be Nosy*, and of course the sign has a very large proboscis. Yes, I'm actually giving you permission to be nosy, to pry into your neighbor's most secretive business. Use any means necessary to sniff it out. Keep in mind that even the most innocent seeming octogenarian can be plotting mayhem of immense proportions. You could be your community's last defense against anarchy. You could also be in big demand at cocktail parties, where you'll of course share all the lurid details you've uncovered.

Finally, the highest level is *Busybody*, symbolized by a buzzing electronic listening device. When the threat reaches this level, you are expected to invest in whatever equipment is needed to invade the privacy and disrupt the lives of any and all members of your community. Wear your busybodyness like a hero's badge. That is what you will be when you take down the terrorist cell that settled into the nondescript split level at the end of Canterbury Court. Absent that, you'll be the cool techy geek who always has the latest toys.

So there you have it: *Aware, Alert, Watch, Nosy, Busybody.* The perfect progression of attentiveness to assure that someone in your neighborhood knows exactly what's going on where, when the threat level is seriously elevated. In many retirement communities, there's already at least one person who does that. I'm simply proposing that we put those proclivities to good use.

I'm confident this system will be as effective as the color-coded one that Homeland Security is jettisoning. As for how it will compare to the new one they're planning... we'll just have to wait and see. It is the federal government, after all.

# Patron Saint of Retirees

Original Post Date Feb. 9, 2011

Retirees have to face a lot of challenges. It seems only fair that we should have a patron saint to guide us and to look out for our interests. I did some research to see if there might already be a patron saint of retirees, but apparently not. This is surprising, considering that there are saints for everything from button makers (Louis IX) to hemorrhoids (Fiacre) to the Internet (Isidore of Seville).

Oh sure, there are patrons for many of the ailments from which retirees often suffer. You've got Ulric for vertigo, and Vitus for over-sleeping (not to be confused with Casanova, for sleeping over). There's even Werenfridus for stiff joints; (try saying his name three times fast without spraying spittle onto your companion). Speaking of stiffs, Stephen the Martyr is the patron saint of casket makers, probably a good one for a retiree to stash in a prayer Rolodex. You might also want to have Saint Christopher on speed dial to assure safe driving into your dotage.

Some ailments have more than one saint whom you can pray to for relief. I found five of them to listen to the pleas of the hearing-impaired, for example, and a wealth of choices (eighteen in all) to receive prayers against impoverishment.

But look for just one to handle the concerns of retirees and your search comes up empty. Is this really so much to ask?

Some saints respond to prayers for an impressive assortment of seemingly unrelated causes. Take John of God, whose patronage extends from heart ailments to alcoholism, but also covers booksellers, firefighters, and hospital workers. Bonaventure is that rarity among patron saints, a specialist; you'll want to call on him to untangle bowel disorders.

The closest saint I could come up with for retirees was Anthony of Padua, patron of the elderly. He's best known for locating lost items, a skill that undoubtedly will come in handy as we move into our golden years. But Anthony already has a list of other causes that would be a handful for even the most experienced saint. Shipwrecks, starvation, sterility, animals, sailors, harvests, paupers, and the oppressed, to name just the more noteworthy ones. No, Anthony must be one busy dude already. He's not likely to have the share of mind available to process the prayers of all the retirees that the baby boom would drop on him.

My husband suggested that FDR would make a great patron saint, because he started Social Security, or alternatively LBJ, because of Medicare—both critical programs in the lives of retirees. I explained to him that in order to be declared a saint, the deceased must be able to take credit for some miracles. While creating Social Security and Medicare may have been miracles in their own right, it doesn't seem likely that people would be comfortable praying to FDR or LBJ to perform miracles in the afterlife. Instead of a halo, their saintly images would no doubt include rings of cigar smoke over their heads. Not to mention, can we be sure they're really up there in heaven and not in... well, you know?

I think a good candidate would be Ethyl Percy Andrus, the founder of AARP. Talk about having the interests of retirees front and center. Fittingly, she died in 1967, the year that the current batch of about-to-be-retirees graduated from college. Since holy folks often take new names in their sainthood, I propose we dub her "Saint Aarpitus," to commemorate the organization she started. We still have to deal with that sticky question of post-death miracles. If any of you have something related to retirement that you feel like praying about, by all means, direct your pleas to Ethyl. If things turn out well for you, let me know. Be sure to have notarized witness statements available for review.

I hate to sound pessimistic—it's not my normal nature, but I think we should have a back-up plan on this. So, until Aarpitus is canonized, I'm going to direct my retirement-related prayers to Saint Jude. I had a bulk rate plan with him during my college years; he's the patron saint of lost causes. When it comes to retirement, you can't get more appropriate than that.

# Retirement Complications— The Chinese Factor

Original Post Date Mar. 5, 2011

Once again I find inspiration for my post in the *Time* magazine that arrived in today's mail. Regular readers of RetirementSparks will have noticed more than an occasional reference to my enjoyment of a nice glass of wine. Preferably red.

There was also my New Year's confession that I don't really drink as much as I make it sound, but that I expect to have more opportunities to sit back with a glass of *vino* once I'm retired. I've even budgeted the added expense—partly under medical, you may recall.

Now comes a wake up call that I may have to redo that budget yet again, and it's all because of what I will call the "Chinese Factor." It seems the Chinese have developed a taste for high-end red wines. According to *Time*, at a recent Sotheby's auction, one bidder from China *"paid $232,000 each for three bottles of 1869 Château Lafite Rothschild."*

I know what you're thinking: *Why should I care?* It's not like buying Château Lafite Rothschild is on my bucket list. Well, you'll want to put a cork in it when you read this next item. At the same auction—held in Hong Kong—someone paid

$70,000 for a case of 2009 Lafite, which hasn't even been bottled yet. According to *Time*, the price represented about a 300% increase over the pre-auction estimate.

On its own, this news would not send me dashing to my retirement spreadsheet. Apparently, the Chinese yen for fine Bordeaux is driving up prices of those wines across the board and around the world. So the Lafite is bound to be just the tip of the wine bottle.

Though my preference is for Italian reds, I will not be lulled into a false sense of security. According to *Time* (or more correctly, Vinexpo, a trade show) Asian wine consumption is growing at four times the global average. You don't get that type of growth without some experimentation—and trickle down. That means price inflation will eventually hit other varieties. Once the Chinese taste a good Barolo, you can forget finding a decent one for under $100 a bottle.

If you hear the phrase "the wine bubble," don't think Asti Spumante, think dotcom. For my sake, and for other wine-loving retirees, we can only hope that the Chinese bubble will burst soon, while wine prices are still where we can afford something other than Night Train. Or Auntie Em's homemade sherry. Blech.

# Crankypants

Original Post Date Apr. 16, 2011

Tina Fey has a new book, *Bossypants*. I haven't read it, but if I ever get a Kindle, it will be the the first book I download. I love Tina Fey, but I don't watch *30 Rock*. It's the *Saturday Night Live* Tina that I love, and not just the Sarah Palin skits. I love the early Tina even more. She's smart. She's funny. She's clever. And she goes toe-to-toe with the big guys in an industry that is about as testosterone saturated as you can get.

If I were to write a book now, it would have to be titled *Crankypants*. I'm just four weeks into retirement, and I can see my patience dwindling day by day. I have never been one to suffer fools gladly, but the freedom of retirement seems to have triggered the hypercritical button in my personality.

I feel free to get annoyed at anything and everything. Simply put, I no longer feel obligated to pretend I'm sociable. Oh, don't look so shocked. What do you expect from someone who sits home drinking wine by herself? Or at least wants you to think she does…

The littlest things annoy me. So, like my pet peeve of the week is the features on morning TV, where the person being interviewed starts every sentence with "so." So, why can't they speak at least one sentence now and then without so much as one "so?" Like, is that so difficult? My second favorite word in these interviews is "like," if you haven't guessed.

I used to be upbeat and positive—a glass half full kind of person. Now, not only do I see the glass as half empty, I find myself inspecting the rim, looking for chips. I know what you're thinking: It's the stress of trying to get the house ready to sell. This is very likely a big part of it. A few nights back, I couldn't sleep, thinking of all that had to be done. I got up and went to the third floor, where I organized and categorized piles of stuff into smaller, neater stacks, including things to throw out. I went back to bed at 3 am.

I keep telling my friends it's like the loaves and the fishes. No matter how much I go through, I don't see any signs of progress. I'm sure that if a stranger walked up to the third floor where I worked until the wee hours, they would ask me: *"When to you plan to start on these rooms?"* When indeed.

I don't really like being cranky, but I don't have the energy to fight it right now. It's easier to be cranky than nice. I never knew that before. There are lots of things I never knew before, most of which have to do with what goes on in my neighborhood on weekdays...

In a nod to my old self, I'm going to end this on an upbeat note. First of all, those of you who've been following the saga of my efforts to start collecting Social Security will be happy to know that everything is now under control. Miss Katshow returned my call—and responded to my certified letter. She claims she never asked for proof of my name change. It was the computer's fault. Apparently, it automatically generates that on line status message when you check the box that says you've ever gone by another name.

Damnable computers. They're to blame for everything that goes wrong in the world. Well, the computers, the religious extremists and the Tea Party. Oh, wait. That's redundant, isn't it… I know I'm not supposed to be ending this cranky, but it's not my fault. The computer made me do it.

Finally, I had fabulous success running errands today. I found an area rug for the third floor landing (wall-to-wall carpet now removed) that couldn't have been better had I designed it myself. Plus it was at a discount store. And I found a replacement cushion for the wicker loveseat for the porch; squirrels and neighborhood cats trashed the old one. The print goes well with the other pillows and it, too, was at a discount store.

After a day like this, there's really not much else to do but sit back, power up the shredder, and pour myself a nice glass of wine. So, if you're not okay with that, you can, like, kiss my crankypants.

# An Archaeological Dig

Original Post Date Apr. 23, 2011

My first weeks of retirement have been spent filing for social security and preparing the house for sale. Both of these projects had me digging through years of accumulated paperwork and belongings, much of it dating back 20 years or more. Several times I went on a quest for one item, only to turn up something else important that I'd given up on. It's as though I've been on an archaeological dig, working my way through layers of past civilizations. Each new level sheds light on my previous lives.

The oldest age I've been able to identify in my dig is what I'll call *"The Formative Years."* I uncovered my grade school report cards, the booklets with my PSAT and SAT scores, my band letter and all three graduation tassels. The band letter is like the ones that athletes earned, but in the shape of a lyre. My report cards reminded me that the only C that I ever received was in fourth grade, for singing. It was not an unfair mark, as anyone who has stood near me at a birthday party during the cake ceremony can attest.

Just above that level, I uncovered memories from my *"Rebel without a Cause"* period. There was my entry for the *Mademoiselle* guest editor competition for college women.

You had to create and produce a new magazine. Mine was titled *Cyclefemme* and featured motorcycles and helmets designed especially for women. I didn't get to be an editor, but I did win a free subscription to *Mademoiselle* for a year.

This overlapped with my *"Hippie"* period, as documented by a photo of me in my Jesus sandals. They had crisscross laces up to my knees and my parents did not approve. One of my aunts had a fancy 50th anniversary party in New Jersey during my senior year in college. I dressed properly for the event, but I changed into traveling clothes for the bus ride back to Rhode Island. When I came out of the rest room to say goodbye, I was wearing my Villager suit with tiny flowers and those sandals. My mother about had apoplexy.

My dig also uncovered *"The Peripatetic Era,"* which occurred mostly in the years right after college. The artifacts from this era included my old passport with all its visas and border crossing stamps. I remember that I had learned to say: *"I have nothing to declare"* in three languages. I also found my travel journal, documenting the places I went with my Eurail Pass, and how much I spent. I lived on an average of $3.40 a day. It was the late sixties.

One of the almost forgotten layers was *"The Jock Age,"* as documented by the forms certifying me to sail solo at the Club Meds in Playa Blanca and Turquoise. Also from one of those vacations—a tank top with a word puzzle on the front and the explanation in French on the back. It got me way more action than my band letter.

Just above that layer, I uncovered the hand-crocheted bikini and gauzy sarong from my *"Exotic Phase."* You'll be forgiven if you confuse this with my *"Gypsy Experiment."* Both involved a lot of head scarves, flowing skirts and large flowers worn in my waist-length hair. (Pictures available for a fee...)

One thing became clear to me as I excavated through the various levels of my existence: the earlier eras seem more interesting than the recent ones. As I look through the layers I've identified, I'm forced to face reality. I wouldn't have the patience to lace up Jesus sandals today. Although I'm still partial to scarves, especially at my neck, my hair is too short to hold flowers. The closest thing to a string bikini that my body could accommodate would be a unitard crafted from compression bandages. (Pictures NOT available, no matter how much you're willing to pay...)

On a brighter note, I expect my retirement years to be full of adventure and excitement. My passport is up to date. I've mastered the art of traveling light. Eurail Passes are still available. I think it may be time to learn to say *"I have nothing to declare"* in a few more languages.

# Apocalypse Prep
Original Post Date May 21, 2011

As if I don't have my hands full enough with retirement planning, I've just become aware of the chatter about the apocalypse happening this Saturday. (That would be today as I post this, but I'm writing it a few days earlier.)

Apparently some dude named Harold Camping has successfully prophesied some events using mathematical calculations that come from the Bible. Now it's telling him that Jesus will return on Saturday and take only the chosen back with Him before He pulls the plug on the rest of us.

I should mention that Camping predicted an earlier end date of September 1994. When we were all still here the next day, he explained that he'd made a math error. In my experience, one math error frequently leads to another. And another. And so on. Not wanting to bet the farm on this, in an effort to assess how real this prophecy might be, I Googled for related news items.

In the *Huffington Post*, I came across the Top 10 Signs the Apocalypse Is Upon Us, written by Dan Tynan and lifted from eSarcasm.com. This is a site and writer I had not been aware of. If you enjoy my style of writing, check out Dan's article. Here's just one of his signs: *"Scientists discover Jupiter-sized 'rogue planets' rolling around the Milky Way like bowling balls in the back of a pickup. You just know one of them is really the Death Star."* Read all ten at http://www.esarcasm.com/21967/top-10-signs-the-apocalypse-is-upon-us/.

A number of sites have bucket lists of things to accomplish before the end of the world, including the venerable Time.com (written by Claire Suddath). *The Daily What* has a flowchart to help you figure out whether you'll be raptured or... It's too painful for me to type the alternative— http://thedailywh.at/2011/05/19/this-x-that-69/.

Even the Centers for Disease Control got into the act. Their post "Preparedness 101: Zombie Apocalypse" (no joke) came out Monday and quickly overwhelmed their servers. Let's hope they get them up again in time for us all to prepare.

Bucket lists and flowcharts aside, I have a handful of urgent decisions to make before midnight Saturday. The first one is: *Will I continue to spell judgment without the middle 'e' the way I was taught in grammar school? Or will I cave in to the increasingly popular misspelling 'judgement'?* If I make the wrong choice, I might not get invited to the rapture party. I wonder: *Will the rapture be like a rave? Or more like a flash mob?* Please, God, don't let it be one big line dance.

Then there are more practical issues. I have a haircut sched-uled Saturday morning. *Should I keep it, so I don't look like wild lady for eternity? Or is it a waste of money at this point?* It's not like I'll be able to take the money with me, and even if I could, where would I spend it? On a related note, my roots are badly in need of coloring. I usually do that on the Sunday evening after the cut. Since I don't know what time we'll be called to judgment, perhaps I should dye my roots before the haircut this time.

Speaking of Sunday, which none of us will see, if the prophe-cy is correct, Sunday is the day I change the litter in the cats' boxes. I should probably change it Saturday morning, just in case. I wouldn't want to send them off into eternity with fouled facilities. I'm a better mother than that. Forced to choose, I'll leave my roots gray and give them clean litter boxes. That alone should earn me a ticket to the rapture.

*Slate* magazine has an interactive feature where you can pick from 144 different scenarios of exactly how the apocalypse will come about. Some examples are loose nukes, space debris and *The Matrix*. If you'd like to review the full list, go to http://www.slate.com/id/2295187/. You can handicap favorites, but there will be small comfort in knowing you were right about how the lights went out.

Okay, rewind a few paragraphs in this post. After some addi-tional searching, I've learned that the chosen will experience their rapture on Saturday on a rolling basis, at 6 PM local in each time zone. Those of us left behind—which will most certainly include me and very likely, many of you, dear readers— will die off gradually due to various calamities that will occur from May 22 through October 21, 2011.

That's the prophesied date of the real blow out Armageddon. It's also the day after our anniversary, so my husband and I have a chance of making it to 21 years. Not quite silver, but we'll take it. After all, one man's Armageddon is another's post-anniversary rapture. If you don't believe me, just ask my husband.

# Charm School
Original Post Date Sep. 10, 2011

There's been a spate of commercials lately for *Barbie's Princess Charm School*. My immediate reaction was concern for the future of feminism. Have we regressed to where little girls have a life goal to become a princess?

My thoughts moved on to charm school topics, so I decided to create *Retirees' Charm School* to make you so irresistible, you'll get invited to more events than a Barbie princess.

## 1. POSTURE.

By the time we retire, we're inclined to... well, actually, we're simply inclined—bent over, that is. A stooped posture makes you look older. Walking with books on your head is still the best exercise for good posture. Collect several months' of AARP magazines for this. They'll bend slightly, shaping to your head's contour, making them easier to balance.

## 2. TABLE MANNERS.

Retirees eat more meals at home than those still working, and we tend to forget about table manners. Then we have our guard down when we do eat out. In addition, our balancing skills deteriorate around retirement. So we raise our plates to our mouths, or bend over so our food is just three inches away. Not charming, and bending over undoes all the good accomplished by walking around with AARPs on your head. Pretend that your spoon contains something you wouldn't want to spill, not even a drop—a fine Barolo wine perhaps. Practice carefully raising the spoon to your mouth while maintaining proper AARP posture. It helps to actually fill the spoon with some primo *vino*.

## 3. PHONE ETIQUETTE.

Retirees are especially subject to telemarketing and robocalls at all hours of the day. Our knee jerk reaction is to snarl some obscenity and hang up. If we're feeling feisty, we give some clever retort, and then hang up. Neither of these reflects the charm we're trying to cultivate.

Instead, inhale deeply, exhale deeply. Count to three slowly. Inhale again, exhale again. Listen for about thirty seconds. (That includes the time you've been inhaling and exhaling.) Then say in your most charming voice, *"You've made some excellent points. Unfortunately, I'm a retiree on very limited income. My time is also limited, since the only way I can make ends meet is to (insert your favorite explanation here.)"* Say a polite goodbye and hang up.

Here are some sample explanations. I have to:

- Crochet toilet paper covers for the church bazaar.
- Stuff envelopes for the Senior Center charity drive.

- Shred Medicare paperwork for everyone in my exercise class.

## 4. FRONT DOOR ETIQUETTE.

This is very similar to phone etiquette, except that you'll be face to face with someone at your front door. It's therefore important to focus on your posture and your facial expression. Be sure to stand tall, so the visitor doesn't think she can bully you. Smile, but not too enthusiastically. Follow the phone etiquette steps, but as part of your polite goodbye, include *"and I really must be getting back to that project now"*, as you gently close the door.

## 5. SENIOR DISCOUNT DAY.

Retirees find themselves able to take advantage of more senior citizens discount days. As a new retiree, you may be offended that no one asks to see your ID. This makes you feel old and cranky and anything but charming. Do not give in to these emotions.

Clerks are used to having people who are not yet seniors claim they are, to get our well-earned discounts. They usually let it slide rather than cause a confrontation. If you look young, the clerk probably just thinks you're a deadbeat. Take it as a compliment and move on. Think back to when you turned 21. You hated having to prove you were old enough to buy a beer. This is simply those chickens coming home to roost.

## 6. DRESSING APPROPRIATELY.

What you wear impacts your charm quotient. As a retiree, your clothing budget is limited. This won't matter if you follow these guidelines.

- Outfits that are charming on pre-teens are eccentric on people over 60.

- Never wear plaid with other plaids. Never wear plaid with floral prints. Come to think of it, just never wear plaid.

- If we can tell it has spandex, you probably should not be wearing it.

- Clip on suspenders are not charming. Get a belt, and not one that leaves 12" hanging.

- If your cords have worn to a shine over your butt, get a new pair.

- God did not intend for us to wear socks with sandals. If your feet are cold even in July, wear shoes.

I could do an entire post on attire, but you get the idea.

Follow these steps and you can charm your way out of trouble and into the best social circles in your neighborhood. I'll bet my plaid spandex jumpsuit on it.

# Retirement Pleasures—Instant Gratification

Original Post Date Oct. 1, 2011

King Abdullah recently announced that women in Saudi Arabia would finally be allowed to vote. My husband enlightened me on the little-reported detail that the change would not take place until 2015. Talk about delayed gratification.

This snippet made me realize that the more comfortable I get in my retirement, the less patience I have with waiting for results, no matter how desirable they may be. I find this ironic, since retirement affords me so much more time to wait for things to happen, or get delivered, or be resolved.

Even the slightest delays annoy me. Take for instance the second or so needed for the newfangled squiggly fluorescent bulbs to light up once you flip the switch. The old incandescent bulbs (which were so much more flattering) went on the instant we summoned them to. Is it so much to ask to "let there be light" as soon as we want it?

You may be thinking: *This is no big deal. What's a little impatience now and then?* Tell that to the tea kettle when I'm standing over it yelling: *"Boil, damn it! Boil!"* Or the washing machine when I'm urging it to *"Spin, already.*

*Spin!"* Inanimate objects have feelings, too, you know. Remember: I'm the hopeless anthropomorphizer.

Don't even get me started on delays that involve phone calls. I've developed a ploy to deal with companies that route me through multi-level menus and then put me on hold for the afternoon. I keep a stack of *New York Times* crossword puzzles nearby, put the phone on speaker and do the puzzles. In my mind, I'm making the company on the other end wait. It may sound silly, but it works for me.

I can't remember the last time I took a rain check for some special that was out of stock at the local market. I never liked them, because I usually lost them before the item came in. Now the very thought of a rain check makes my nostrils flare.

This need for instant gratification probably explains why you don't see women over sixty who are pregnant. We'd never have the patience to wait nine months for the blessed event. I can barely tolerate the thirty-five minutes for a pizza delivery.

My retirement has had the side benefit that I have little need for new clothes. This is a good thing, because my width-to-height ratio invariably requires alterations. Jacket sleeves shortened a tad, pants shortened a lot. When an event calls for new clothes, I have to plan at least two weeks between purchase and actual use. In my retirement, two weeks is an eternity, and my patience has already been shortened to the max.

You can imagine what a joy I am to be with when I'm stuck in traffic. The good news is that I've made a habit of learning alternate routes and back roads. More often than not, I'm able to avoid sitting at a total stand still. The travel time might be longer than planned, but at least I'm moving. It's certainly better than hyperventilating through a major delay on the primary route, chanting "om, om, om."

Websites that take forever to load are dead on arrival. I close the window and start over somewhere else. Likewise huge email attachments. There's nothing I'd want to see on my computer screen that's worth waiting for, except pictures of my grandnieces and grandnephew. Their parents know to send these low res, but I'd even take a rain check for them.

My newfound antsiness helps me appreciate Twitter's appeal. With messages limited to 140 characters, communications are almost instantaneous. Bantering is as rat-a-tat as a tennis rally between top ranked players. I say this with no personal knowledge. Although I signed up for a Twitter account and made one maiden tweet, I don't use it. The text option on our cell phones costs extra, and I'm saving my thumbs for more important things—like leafing through crossword puzzles and jiggling the light switch.

I'd like to think this is just a phase I'm going through, and that in a year or so, I'll have mellowed out. Maybe. But I doubt I can wait that long to find out.

# Section VI

# Miscellaneous Musings
# On Retirement

# Too Many Changes
Original Post Date Jan. 22, 2011

I'm expecting a lot of changes to come along with retirement, but this past week or so has been flooded with changes that have nothing to do with my impending transition. It's just too much to wrap my brain around all at once.

Watching *Live with Regis and Kelly* was not top of the list of things I planned to do once I'll be home during the day. But this week, Regis Philbin announced he's stepping down from his co-hosting spot of about ninety years. This, on top of Oprah shutting down her show, has me worried that there may be nothing left on daytime TV about which I can feel smug for not watching.

Then there's the new size drink that Starbucks is offering. It's called a Trenta and it's 31 ounces, or 50 percent bigger than their previous mouthful, the Venti. I'm not a coffee drinker, but I occasionally have a cup of tea at Starbucks. It took me several trips to figure out the Venti, but now it sounds like the Trenta may be a good size for iced tea. Meanwhile, rumor has it that they are about to introduce yet another size, to commemorate all the baby boomers who will soon be retiring. This new 65-ounce drink will be called the Sessanta, but it will be nicknamed the "bladder buster." Can't wait.

The ultimate blow however, is the news that I am no longer a Virgo. Yup. Some astronomer in Minnesota pointed out that since the signs of the Zodiac were based on the earth's relationship to the sun, they went out of whack hundreds of years ago. It has something to do with the earth's orbit around the sun changing slightly every year. The proposed new Zodiac would make me a Leo, not quite on the cusp of Virgo. This is very upsetting to me, as I've always recognized myself as a classic Virgo. Much as I love felines, I'm not sure I'll be comfortable in the skin of a lion. And no snide comments about my fitting in a virgin's skin, thank you.

I shouldn't really complain. The poor folks born between November 29 and December 17 now have a new sign altogether. It's called Ophiuchus, which means "the serpent-bearer." The symbol is not at all appealing, but the name sounds positively obscene. And I ask you crossword puzzle fans out there, have you ever done a puzzle that had Ophiuchus as the answer to "constellation around the celestial equator"?

What could be a problem, though, is that my husband is now smack in the middle of Sagittarius. I have no idea if that sign is compatible with Leo. We had our charts cast before we married, to make sure we were well-suited to one another. All boded well for the union of a Virgo and a Capricorn. I guess we'll have to get our charts redone to make sure we should stay together after 20 years.

My optimistic self says we're probably still well-aligned. But given all the upheaval from this week, it would be just my luck to find out I should be spending my time with an Ophiuchus. The one-time virgin matched with a man with a serpent... Talk about Freudian symbolism. That prospect calls for a fresh bottle of wine...

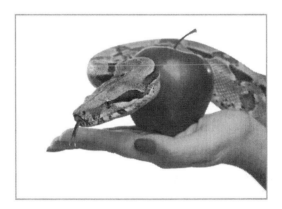

# More on the New Zodiac

Original Post Date Jan. 26, 2011

Those of you who read my last post and were worried about whether my husband and I would still be compatible under the revised Zodiac can rest easy. I looked up Leo and Sagittarius in Linda Goodman's *Love Signs*. Best I can tell, we're as well-suited to each other as a lioness and an archer as we were when I was the virgin and he was the goat. That is to say, not the best astrological match, but once we understand one another's quirks, we can work things out if we're willing to put in some effort.

This is a good thing, not just because it means I won't have to go looking for a new partner as I retire, and hence dealing with yet more change in my life. You may recall that I was worried that the stars would point toward a pairing of Leo with that new sign, Ophiuchus, and I've uncovered some disturbing qualities about Ophiuchus.

Ophiuchi are known to be doctors; the caduceus, or medical staff, is based on their serpent. They're also supposedly good interpreters of dreams and have vivid premonitions. In my book, that combination spells "shrink." Given how weird my dreams have been lately, I'm not sure it would be a good idea to have someone poking around in them looking for meaning.

Supposedly Ophiuchi are flamboyant dressers and are drawn to bright colors, especially plaids. (Go figure.) They're described as eccentric and quirky, but I blame that on the flamboyant plaids, especially for males of this sign. They've also been called fun-loving, with magnetic personalities, but I'm guessing it's those plaids again that draw the crowds around them. Or it could be that lyre they're always plunking away on.

My sleuthing has uncovered another little known trait of this new Zodiac sign. Turns out, they have an unhealthy attraction to their parent of the opposite sex. Bad things have been known to happen, especially to fathers of male Ophiuchi, who (ironically) are supposedly favored by their dads and other authority figures. In yet another display of irony, Ophiuchi dislike authority and regulations. In other words, they are generally members of the Tea Party.

There seem to be a lot of contradictions surrounding those born under this new sign. On the one hand, they're credited with having a lot of creativity, imagination and curiosity. On the other, they're supposedly lazy and prone to procrastination. Likewise, though fun-loving, they're also described as prone to bouts of depression. Some fun. Maybe they should pair with one another, so they could deconstruct each other's dreams to figure out why they're in the dumps.

Which brings me to the two absolute deal breakers as far as pairing me with an Ophiuchus. They're not big on monogamous relationships. The last thing I need as I drift off into retirement is a philandering partner. If I didn't actually kill him, I'd certainly dream about it. And the wine bills would bankrupt me.

And finally, Ophiuchi dislike irrelevant and trivial information. Here I stand, the master of the trivial, the lover of a meandering stroll down a side path of irrelevant recollection. No, I could never abide a partner from that Zodiac sign. Give me my new Sagittarius—or my old Capricorn. I'm more than willing to put in the effort to keep it working with him, quirks and all.

# New Astronomy

Original Post Date Feb. 16, 2011

The closer I get to retirement, the less I'm a fan of change. Don't get me wrong. I'm willing to try new things, if they are cutting edge and provide something no one ever thought of before. Even better if they solve some problem I didn't know I had. What I don't like is change for no defensible reason, or for no reason other than to line someone else's pockets.

I recently posted about the new astrology, the results of which changed me from a Virgo to a Leo, and my husband from a Capricorn to a Sagittarius. I wasn't happy about that change. I liked being the virgin with a spouse who was always the goat. Now I've discovered that I have to come to terms with the new astronomy, too.

There are, of course, two kinds of astronomy, the literal and the figurative. We all understand the figurative. On the show *The Honeymooners*, Ralph Cramden was always threatening to send Alice "to the moon." Even as a child, I knew that was just a figure of speech. I didn't expect to see Alice perched on a shining crescent in the sky one night. When I fell out of the tree I was climbing as a youngster, I said I saw stars, and when my first boyfriend finally kissed me, I was on cloud nine. No one took me literally.

When the figurative meaning of an astronomical reference changes, it doesn't affect our lives much. But when astronomy changes literally, as it has recently, it takes some work to keep up. Case in point, you must have heard that Pluto was demoted from planet status to a dwarf in 2006. Those of us who had memorized the mnemonic MVEMJSUNP *(My Very Energetic Mother Just Served Us Nine Pizzas)* had to come up with a new way to remember the order of the remaining eight. Something like: *My Very Energetic Mother Just Served Us Nincompoops.* Not the best use of our time, in my opinion.

Sometimes the literal and the figurative overlap. For most of our lives, my brother-in-law and I rarely agreed on much. The older we get, however, the more we find ourselves nodding when the other says something. It's confounding the rest of our family. Recently when he said something relatively conservative and I announced that I thought he was right, the entire roomful of relatives moved to the window in swarm-like fashion, to see if there was a bright star in the mid-day sky that they should follow somewhere. Their expectations were figurative, but the star they were looking for was literal. If the room had been a boat, it would have capsized.

Here's another example that comes to mind, especially when we think of retirees. How many of us have friends who tell us they're "heading to the sun"? They probably don't mean they've reserved a spot on a Virgin Galactic space shuttle (though over 390 "astronauts" have done so already.) They are in fact heading closer to the sun, however, most likely to Florida for the winter, and probably to a condo that cost a bit more than the shuttle ticket's $200,000.

Finally—and this is what prompted me to write this post—I return to my earlier spot on cloud nine. Turns out, people mean something very different now when they say they are going "to the cloud." They mean it literally, or at least as literally as the friends who are heading to the sun. "Cloud" is a metaphor for the Internet, based on the symbol used to represent it. But it also refers to real services that are delivered literally over the Internet.

I decided to find out more about the new astronomy of the cloud. Here's some of what I learned. It's a general term for delivering hosted services over the Internet. The National Institute of Standards and Technology (NIST) describes cloud computing as *"enabling convenient, on-demand network access to a shared pool of configurable computing resources."*

You can go to the cloud even if you have no knowledge of where it is physically—What, it's not up in the sky?—or how its system is configured. So all that Mac/PC/Linux nonsense goes away. Sorry, admen. All you need is your personal computer, a functioning web browser, and Internet access. This last item may be the biggest challenge any of us face in getting to the cloud.

As appealing as this sounds, I don't think I'll be going there anytime soon. You see, I also learned something scary about the cloud: it can be public. In my mind, I'm back on my comfortable spot on cloud nine. I can tell you this: no way on God's green acre do I want anything there to be shared publicly. If I wanted the whole world to have access to what I'm doing on my cloud, I'd post it on Facebook. Simply put, WHOCNSOCN. *(What Happens On Cloud Nine, Stays On Cloud Nine.)*

# Retirement Pleasures—Reciprocity
Original Post Date Feb. 23, 2011

When I actually retire, I expect to spend more time on Facebook. I don't mean that I'll become addicted to it or start playing Farmville. I just assume that I'll check my home page more regularly and weigh in more often with my two cents in the comment threads.

I first got involved with Facebook for business reasons; hard to believe, I know. I thought the nonprofit I head up should be on Facebook, but I wanted to learn more about it before I put their reputation at risk. I also felt it would be helpful to begin to amass a network of potential followers for the web-based projects I hope to develop once I retire.

I quickly realized that it can be fun to reconnect with friends from my distant past—from high school, even grade school. I took the time to complete a fairly thorough profile and all sorts of people began to find me. Then came my birthday and an in-box full of greetings, some from folks I barely knew. That's when I discovered the birthday alert feature, and along with it, the merits of reciprocity.

Once a week, I receive an email from the Wizard of Facebook with a list of people in my network who have birthdays in the upcoming week. I make it a point to send greetings, even to those who are only vague acquaintances. I do this, because I remember how happy I was to get similar messages, and I've discovered that reciprocating makes me feel warm and fuzzy inside.

This applies to comments on blog posts, as well. Several friends read my posts, some quite regularly, but very few post their own comments. Every now and then, someone I don't know stumbles across RetirementSparks and posts a thoughtful or encouraging remark. Sometimes I can trace who they are and I discover that they, too, have a blog. If so, I link through, read some of their writings and post a comment of my own. I feel that it's important to reciprocate, to support my fellow bloggers.

Reciprocity is different from paying it forward. You reciprocate as part of an anticipated exchange of thoughtfulness, a back and forth. Tit for tat, if you will; please, no snickering. For example, my friend, Becky, travels a lot and sometimes asks me to water her plants. My husband, Jagdish, and I are rarely away from home at the same time, but I can count on Becky to feed our cats, if need be. Giving Lily her pill is another story altogether.

As I was lying in bed one night last week, a variation on the Mercy speech from *The Merchant of Venice* kept running through my mind. *"The quality of reciprocity is not strain'd...*" You need to want to reciprocate for it to work its magic. *"It blesseth him that gives and him that takes."* That's the Facebook birthday thing, in the bard's words.

I've decided that retirement will be a good time to invest in more reciprocity. Here are some ideas that come to mind right out of the gate. I plan to get more exercise once I retire, and walking is a good way to start. I know I'll do it more regularly if I have someone to do it with. So, if Fred calls and says *"Do you want to walk this morning?"* I'll say *"Sure!"* even if I'd rather put my feet up and sip Earl Grey. This is because I know that if I decide to walk at 7 one evening, I'll call him and say, *"I need to take a walk, and I'd like some company"* and he'll come along to reciprocate.

My sister and I have already made an arrangement whereby we'll pluck the goat hairs from one another's chins when our eyesight is too far gone for us to do it our own. Now that's merciful reciprocity.

Once we retire, I expect that Jagdish and I will put cream on the dry spots on one another's backs. I do his at bedtime now, but he rarely reciprocates. I prefer to moisturize in the morning, and he's usually still in the shower when I dress for work. When I retire, I expect to have skin as soft as a baby's bum.

If I put my mind to it, I know I'll come up with dozens of ways to experience the pleasure of reciprocity, and none of them involving sex—although that's also an option, I suppose, what with my newly soft skin. The ways I uncover are more likely to be practical ones. Maybe things to do with household chores, or kitchen-related tasks.

I can almost hear me now. *"Honey, I'll unscrew the lid on your peanut butter jar if you'll pull the cork out of my wine bottle."* I propose a new proverb: *Blessed be the reciprocators, for theirs is the kingdom of retirement.*

# Blessed Are They

Original Post Date Feb. 26, 2011

Someone pointed out that the proverb with which I ended my previous post was more of a beatitude. Not surprisingly, this got me to thinking that those who are retired deserve to have a set of beatitudes all their own. And more than eight of them. So herewith are my Retirement Beatitudes.

* Blessed are they who have suffered through preparing Medicare Part A and Part B applications, for their health care shall be covered by Plan A (or was it Plan B?)

* Blessed are they who are already on Social Security, for they shall obtain their benefits from a secure lock box.

* Blessed are they whose knees have succumbed to arthritis, for they shall possess robotic replacements.

* Blessed are they who are losing their sense of balance, for they shall be lifted upon the wings of angels—or else on a really good walker.

* Blessed are they who are on statins, for their arteries shall not get clogged with plaque, provided they stop eating deep fried foods and cut down on saturated fats.

* Blessed are they who downsized to a condominium, for they shall have their lawns mowed and their snow cleared for them.

* Blessed are they who serve on their neighborhood watch, for they shall be known by where they live and someone will direct them there if they get lost.

* Blessed are they who volunteer in their community, for they shall be called "goody two shoes" even if they wear orthopedic oxfords.

* Blessed are they who had the foresight (and financial wherewithal) to purchase long term care insurance, for their children shall inherit their estates.

* Blessed are they who have signed do-not-resuscitate orders, for they shall not burden our beneficent government (and their fellow taxpayers) by being put on life support when their mental faculties have gone on to greener pastures.

* Blessed are they who do crossword puzzles and sudokus, for they... oh, dear. I forget why they shall be blessed.

* Blessed are they who do not complain to their spouses all day long and drive them crazy when they stop working, for they shall not be suffocated under a pillow in the dead of night.

That makes an even dozen and you didn't have to go to the Mount to receive them. So I think my job is done for today, except for one more thing: *Bless you!*

# Retirement Commandments—
# Judeo-Christian Version

Original Post Date Mar. 12, 2011

Since the posts on Retirement Beatitudes and the Patron Saint of Retirees were so well received, I give you today the Ten Retirement Commandments, Judeo-Christian style. (*"Thou shalt nots."*)

1. Thou shalt not tell thy successor how to do thy job, as it is no longer thine.

2. Thou shalt not pester thy former colleagues every day for information on how things are going at thy old office. (See commandment #1.)

3. Thou shalt not taunt pre-retirees on their way to work each morning. Remember: Their paychecks are generating the contributions that are helping to keep Social Security solvent.

4. Thou shalt not bear false witness about how thou spent thy day, trying to make it sound more productive or exciting. It is what it is. Or was.

5. Thou shalt not commit line dancing, no matter how itchy thy feet may get when the music starts. Thou might as well carry a huge placard that reads "Retiree with no life."

6. Thou shalt not engage in competitions with fellow-retirees to see who can grow the biggest tomatoes (or squash, or sunflowers, or… thou gets the idea).

7. Thou shalt not embarrass thy pets by dressing them up in cute little outfits to break up the monotony. If thou art bored in thy retirement, take thee up a hobby.

8. Thou shalt not crochet tacky tissue and toilet paper covers to give to thy friends. This is not what we had in mind when we said "hobby." (See commandment #7.)

9. Thou shalt not covet thy neighbor's pension (or condo, or vegetable garden, or… thou gets the idea). (See commandment # 6.)

10. Thou shalt not succumb to the temptations of the phish (spoofs to get your personal info for illegal purposes), Thou dost not have a long lost uncle who became a missionary in Nigeria. Do not send his widow money, no matter how poignant her email may be. Tell her thou art on a fixed income with no discretionary spending. Thou shalt not be lying.

I could go on, but since the original came in a set of ten, it seems respectful to keep this list at ten as well.

# Retirement Commandments— Zoroastrian Version

Original Post Date Mar. 16, 2011

My husband—Hindu by birth—pointed out to me that the Zoroastrian version of commandments states everything in the positive, not the negative (more *"thou shalt"* than *"thou shalt not."*) So, in a nod to ecumenism, here are the Zoroastrian Retirement Commandments.

1. Thou shalt establish a daily routine and adhere to it. Thou shalt be sure to include time for spontaneity, ideally from 11 am to noon and from 7:30 to 8 pm.

2. Prepare thee a budget and keep thee to it, no matter how cute the red shoes are that thou finds on sale. Know thee that "sexy orthopedics" is an oxymoron.

3. Honor thy social security, for thou might be the last generation to get it.

4. Thou shalt alter thy grocery shopping schedule to coincide with Senior Discount Day. If thou hast a choice in stores, thou shalt go to the one that asks for proof of age, telling thee thou cannot possibly be a senior citizen.

5. Thou shalt exercise every day and shalt include aerobics and weight bearing exercises. Getting out of bed and climbing in and out of the bathtub count as weight bearing exercises. Shaking all night long from restless leg syndrome and slipping and falling in the shower are considered aerobic activity.

6. Gather around thee thy family and friends for mutual support, such as plucking each other's chin hairs. If thou relocates, thou shalt find new friends, preferably ones with good eyesight and steady hands.

7. Thou shalt faithfully take thy vitamins and daily medication as prescribed by thy physician. Remember to include thy liquid vitamins—especially red ones in green glass bottles.

8. Beware of false prophets promising extraordinary profits. Retirement is no time for high risk ventures (or low rise pants).

9. Speak respectfully of thine elders, no matter how bizarre their behavior, for some day thou might become one of them.

10. Thou shalt prepare a to-do list for each day. Thou shalt then proceed to do absolutely nothing that is on the to-do list. That is what retirement is all about.

All these commandments are important, but the tenth is most important. If you choose to obey only one, follow that one . I, however, will be sure to obey number 7. Surprise, surprise.

# Retirement Tools—An App for That

Original Post Date Mar. 30, 2011

Retirement is a time when it makes sense to adopt new technology; it can make our lives so much easier. Fortunately, we have plenty of time to become familiar with new things. Unfortunately, the E-Trade baby is more tech savvy than much of the generation that witnessed Woodstock and Watergate. He even has more hair than many of us.

Among the newer tools are the apps for smart phones. For those out of touch with the lingo, "app" is short for "application," not "aptitude," but you do need some skill to use these. My cell phone is stupid; it's for emergencies and travel and has a 100 minute per month limit. I never text; that costs extra. I don't even know if the phone takes pictures.

Nonetheless, when I hear: *"There's an app for that,"* it piques my curiosity. So, for those with phones that are smarter than mine—which would be most, if not all, of you, I've researched some of the newest, coolest, most useful apps for retirees.

The first of these is Apple's Find My iPhone, which gives you a map showing where your phone is. It's not clear how a map on the phone you can't find can help you locate that phone.

However, I have it on good authority that variations will be available shortly that will pinpoint your car in a multi-story parking garage and your reading glasses anywhere in your house, including on top of your head. Now those are apps that retirees are waiting for.

Another good app is Word Lens. The original was developed to translate printed material between English and Spanish. You'll want to get the up 'til now top secret "big print" version, which is in beta testing. Point your smart phone at any printed info and it will magnify it to the level you've specified. This will be especially helpful if you've misplaced your reading glasses and don't have the Find My Glasses app. As your eyesight gets progressively worse, just key in the new magnification and you're back in business. That's an app worth getting a smart phone for.

If you're a retirochondriac (see post in Section I), you'll want the WebMD app to search your symptoms. Few people know about its companion MedAlert app that tracks down your physician with an emergency page. The app is smart enough to figure out which doctor from your lengthy contact list handles the condition involved. I don't know about you, but sometimes I'm not sure who handles what in my healthcare.

The gardeners among you will want the Weed Wacker app. Snap a photo of any emerging greenery—or brownery. The app will tell you whether to pull it, pluck it, mulch it or fertilize it. The game Trade Nations is described as *"best played in short, productive bursts."* Talk about an app made in heaven for retirees. I wish my entire day could be spent in short, productive bursts. Puzzle Agent promises an *"engrossing experience"* that combines *"classic adventure games with thought-provoking puzzles."* I've reached the age where most puzzles are engrossing or thought-provoking. I don't need an app for that.

Many apps do price comparisons, but I decided to check out Budget Police. With most retirees on fixed budgets, it sounded like a sure winner. You key in your weekly spending allocation and your proposed shopping list. It prioritizes your purchases and tells you where to get them at the best price. If your list goes over budget, it deletes the items it decides you don't need. I did a test run with Budget Police. It deleted the wine off my list and said I was over quota for the month. You can be sure I won't be upgrading to a smart phone to get an app that tells me I can't buy wine.

N.O.V.A.2, a game app, arms you with futuristic powers, like slowing down time, an invaluable tool for a retiree. I hear that N.O.V.A.3 (due out next year) will enable you to aim your phone at any part of your body and relieve the symptoms of arthritis. N.O.V.A.4 (still under development) will work similarly, but will burn off fat. I'm on the advance purchase list for that. If it works, I'd like to join the Artisanal Chocolate of the Month Club. I wonder if there's an app for that...

# Venice Expo as Metaphor

Original Post Date Jun. 8, 2011

The inspiration for today's post came from the *New York Times* review of the 54th Biennale in Venice, one of the world's most respected art expositions. What caught my eye was the headline: "Old Patina Encircles Fresh Art in Venice."

My immediate thought was: *"I know what they mean. I feel like I'm an old patina encircling the young people I meet, now that I'm retired."* Not surprisingly, I was motivated to read the entire article. Talk about a treasure trove of metaphors for retirement! Let me give credit in advance to *Times* contributor, Carol Vogel, for being such a rich source of material and for my liberal excerpts from her write-up.

In her first paragraph, Ms. Vogel describes this Biennale as *"more subdued and less experimental"* than past ones. Compare my years immediately post-college with my current life and you'll find that phrase is an appropriate subtitle for my autobiography. Vogel also calls the expo *"a nostalgic meditation on life,"* which could be a generic subtitle for almost any retiree's reflections.

The Biennale's curator, Bice Curiger, installed 16th century Venetian art at the expo's entrance, specifically, works by

Tintoretto. She described the *"demolition of a static order, the loss of harmony"* in his "Last Supper," as evidenced by the fact that *"Christ is no longer at the center of the scene, and the table lies diagonally across the painting."*

If that isn't a metaphor for my retirement, I'll eat my AARP membership card. I've come to terms with the fact that I'm now more likely to be on the sidelines of events than at the center. And I readily confess that if you put me anywhere near a horizontal surface about an hour after I've had lunch, you're likely to find me lying diagonally across it before the mail has been delivered.

The Biennale has been described as bigger than ever, which is exactly what my internist found when he weighed me at my recent checkup. To use his words at the end of our semi-annual get together: *"Your blood pressure's fine. You're generally in good health. It's just that there's too much of you."* Speaking of which...

One of Vogel's more colorful items about the expo is her description of Jeff Koons's sculpture "Fait d'Hiver," as *"a busty porcelain woman in a fishnet top being ogled by a porcelain pig and penguin."* Now that's cutting a little too close to home. Oh, wait. It says "busty," not "buttsy."

And while we're close to home, some of the language reminds me of my house during the staging process. Per

Vogel, the Biennale had many off-site exhibits, *"stuffed into abandoned churches, disused palaces and empty industrial buildings."* Or as I'd like to say of my belongings that the Realtors' stager banished: *"Stuffed into abandoned storage trunks, disused closets and empty drawers."* Fishnet stockings, anyone?

Japanese artist Tabaimo said his exhibit was about *"receding into isolation in the face of globalization."* There are days when government functionaries and multinational corporations have me thinking Tabaimo is on to something, but the last thing I want to become is a hermit curmudgeon. There are already some role models for that in my life, and they're not what Martha Stewart would call "a good thing."

A similarly glass-half-empty point of view was expressed in the environmental commentary of Swiss artist, Thomas Hirschhorn. His installation was comprised of old computer screens, cell phones, plastic chairs and such, reflecting *"a world of high-speed obsolescence."* I have nothing to say about fellow Swiss artist, Pipilotti Rist. I just love the name and wanted to include it in this post.

I prefer to focus on the commentaries of the glass-half-full members of the art world. Thomas P. Campbell, director of the Metropolitan Museum of Art, reportedly enjoyed the exposition, describing it as *"chaotic, kaleidoscopic and exciting."* That sounds a lot more like the life I aspire to lead once

I settle fully into retirement. I could do without the chaotic part, but I'm a realist. No matter how much I declutter and downsize, it's unlikely I'll completely escape chaos.

Vogel ended her review with a quote from Richard Armstrong, director of the Solomon R. Guggenheim Foundation, reflecting on the Hirschhorn installation. He described it as *"an elegy toward postindustrialism."* His poetic observation: *"As we glide into the simulated universe, real things take on a different, maybe even talismanic significance."*

Now there's a thought I can sink my mental teeth into: real things becoming talismans in my retirement. So, if you'll excuse me, I'm going to pour a generous glass of wine and glide off into a simulated universe. Preferably one without a porcelain pig.

# Crazyville

Original Post Date Jun. 4, 2011

The end of this week finds me worrying that we relocate to Crazyville around the time we reach retirement age. Take for example the news item about the 73 year old man from Southern Arizona who was so insane over the terms of his latest divorce that he went on a shooting rampage.

At the end of it, his ex-wife and her lawyer were both dead, as were three bystanders and the man himself. His death was a suicide. Apparently he built up his courage by practicing on the other victims. He had certainly practiced the divorce part, having been through four of them before calling it quits with the wife he shot. It's unclear whether he tried to shoot any of his other exes.

I know what you're thinking: *"It must have been a hell of a divorce settlement."* Actually, the main issue was who got custody of their mobile home. The article did not specify whether it was a double-wide. The marriage lasted from 2002 to 2007, which made the shooter 64 to 69 during the union.

What made him go berserk this time around? Why now, if they split in 2007? Was the trailer that fabulously tricked out? Perhaps by the time he reached 73, this man from a farming community near Yuma had inhaled too much fertilizer. I think he simply moved closer to Crazyville as he got older.

Here's another news item from the *New York Times*. A former Wall Street trader took his own life just a few days after one of his secretly taped conversations had been played in court. It supposedly implicated him in insider trading and the tape had been used to secure his cooperation in spying on his peers for the FBI.

His wife said he was *"conflicted about his cooperation," "worried about entrapping his friends"* and depressed over losing his job—his employer had found out about the spying. This alone could explain why a 50 year old would hop on the train to Crazyville, but wait—there's more.

Before agreeing to turn snitch, the man sought legal advice. His attorney counseled him to cooperate, but to tell no one else (again per the *Times*) except his rabbi and his (nonexistent) therapist. His attorney is now a chief assistant DA. Yet another example of a lawyer who helped punch the ticket to ride to suicide.

At least the trader didn't kill his wife or others before he hung himself. Had he been ten years older, he would have been a lot closer to Crazyville and it would have ended with a lot more mess. The assistant DA should say his "thank you" prayers that the trader was fired and not retired.

My initial vetting of Realtors had me dangerously close to reserving a seat on that Crazy train. (Is the market THAT bad?) The week ended better than it appeared it would. The second Realtors I interviewed came in with figures extremely close to the ones I'd put together and they had considerable data to support their proposal. That was the good news.

The bad news is their laundry list of things to fix. Beyond the financial consequences, there's the net result that I won't be able to list the house for at least two more weeks. Say good-bye to any buyers who want to close before their kids' school terms begin.

On top of that, the agents brought their stager to tell me what more I need to thin/rearrange before anyone sees my gem of a home. Once again, the good news: I feel we'll work well together. The bad news: I have about one third more furniture than he envisions being here when the house is ready to show.

Obviously, I plan to sell/donate a fair amount before we move, but I can't stop my prepping to hold a tag sale. Where do the entertainment unit, tall curio cabinet, highboy chest, small TV cabinet, second sideboard, six high chairs and four doll carriages go in the meantime? And that's just the larger items. I'm sure I'll figure this out, but for the moment, it leaves me in a very precarious state of mind.

This is a dangerous place to be when one's real estate agent says this about the listing process: *"Once you put your house on the market, it no longer belongs to you; it belongs to the public."* Public indeed.

Fair warning to my husband: next stop Crazyville. Though I haven't been dealing with any attorneys (yet), I have a feeling real estate agents will face the same risks once I get on that train.

Unless of course there's a bar car that serves good quality red wine.

# Reasons to Watch TV

Original Post Date Jun. 29, 2011

As if I didn't already watch too much TV, tonight's news gives me two more reasons to become a couch potato.

The first is my own logical extension of a study published in the *Journal of Public Economics*. It shows that more people die within a few days of when they get paid than at any other time. Note that getting paid includes receiving Social Security checks and tax refunds, so this applies to retirees as well as those still gainfully employed.

The author's assumption is that people go out to spend some of that money, making them more prone to auto accidents or other misadventures, the result of engaging in risky business of one sort or another.

My monthly payments get auto-deposited, but just to be safe, I'm going to make it a point to stay home and watch TV during those high-risk days. This should improve my odds of avoiding payday demise.

The other piece of news was an update on technology that will enable TVs to emit specific aromas. This capability has been around for awhile, but apparently not in a refined enough way to make it commercially viable. As with most things, give them enough time, and they'll figure it out.

"They" in this case is the team of Samsung and the University of California San Diego, who have developed a device to deliver 10,000 distinct aromas. These are chemically created, of course, but then so are most of the fragrances in our soaps and other health and beauty aids. You didn't honestly think that purplish goo was made from real lavender, did you?

The TV device works via a matrix of 100 X 100 little cells. Yet another practical application for an Excel spreadsheet... Each cell contains a minute solution that, when heated, turns to gas. That gas delivers the specific smell. I assume these can also be combined, much the way a fragrance house mixes scents, especially since it was tested using perfumes that carry the names of two celebrities. Test subjects could tell the difference from 10 feet away.

Attach this little sucker to your TV set and the next thing you know, you're smelling the garlic in that garlic and citrus chicken dish Giada de Laurentiis is cooking up. Or maybe it will be her perfume. I'll bet she smells fabulous. She certainly looks great. (Are you guys out there drooling over the chicken or the eggplants?)

The latest developments in this technology were reported in a paper published in *Angewandte Chemie*, the journal of the

German Chemical Society. I love the name of this journal almost as much as I love the name Pipilotti Rist, the Swiss artist I mentioned in my post on the Venice Biennale earlier in this section.

Yes, dear readers, the day when TV advertisers will manipulate us through our noses and not just our eyes will soon be upon us. We may as well embrace the new technology. At least it will keep us off the highway and away from all those high-risk behaviors we all crave the minute our Social Security payments hit the bank. Thank you and *zum wohl*, Samsung, UCSD and *Angewandte Chemie*. I raise my glass to all of you. And by the way, can you please set the cell E6 to have the aroma of a fine Barolo?

# Ice Cream for Retirees

Original Post Date Jul. 16, 2011

A special on *The View* alerted me to the fact that July is National Ice Cream Month, so designated by President Reagan in 1984. The special featured what can only be described as an orgy of sampling exotic flavors from ice cream purveyors around the country. The flavors included such unusual ingredients as bacon, jalapeno and alcoholic spirits like whiskey and vodka.

Not to be outdone, I've scoured the countryside to find ice cream flavors developed specifically to appeal to the senior palat—and digestive system. You won't find these on *The View's* website. In fact, you won't find them anywhere except *RetirementSparks*. In celebration of National Ice Cream Day—which is the third Sunday of July—here are the top ten flavors for the over-fifty crowd.

### 1. Apple Sauce

A perennial favorite, this is made with a vanilla base and has swirls of Granny Smith applesauce with just a hint of cinnamon. This flavor is rumored to be the source of the expression *"How do you like them apples?"* but we wouldn't bank on it.

## 2. Oatmeal Delight

Another popular flavor, Oatmeal Delight has a low fat vanilla base, with clumps of oatmeal, whole raisins and a soupçon of nutmeg blended into the perfect texture. Enjoy it morning, noon or night. Guilt free.

## 3. Prune Whip

This over-fifty choice has a butter cream base with pureed prunes swirled throughout. It's double churned for extra air, extra lightness, extra… never mind.

## 4. Liver Spots

This is another vanilla-based treat, this time with carob chips throughout. It was originally served at Patricia Murphy's in New York City and was named for how it looks, not how it tastes. It's still available in selected restaurants, but only until 5 PM.

## 5. Maalox

Immediately recognizable by its bubble gum pink color, this is a combination of strawberry and peppermint. You'll love the soothing way it coats your tummy. It's best eaten slowly and in small spoonfuls.

## 6. Fiberberry

A conglomeration of the more popular berries, this flavor has a peach base and a generous amount of blueberries, blackberries and strawberries mixed throughout. Be sure to have toothpicks and floss at the ready, so you can pick out all those little seeds that will be left in your teeth. Did we mention you'll be getting your daily requirement of fiber in one generous serving?

## 7. Blazing Curry

Made with ghee (India's clarified butter), this curry ice cream was created especially for arthritis sufferers. It's loaded with turmeric and has a serious amount of cayenne, agents known to relieve pain. As an added benefit, smoosh it into a Zip Loc bag and place it directly on your knees for instant relief.

## 8. Bananayama

One of the most mellifluously named flavors for seniors, this banana-based treat has honey-laced yams mashed throughout. High in potassium and anti-oxidants, richly colored, Bananayama is simply the bees knees.

## 9. Sorbet Surprise

For those who are lactose intolerant, this tangy sorbet made especially for those over fifty is a special treat. It's non-dairy and has a surprise in the middle of each scoop. We'd tell you what that is, but then it wouldn't be a surprise, would it.

10. Decaf Espresso

This flavor has all the intensity of Espresso, but with the caffeine removed. You can eat an entire quart after dinner and still fall asleep at 9 PM. In case that's important to you.

That rounds out our list of ten ice cream flavors especially for seniors. Be sure to have a big scoop of something rich and creamy and icy cold on National Ice Cream Day. Do it for the Gipper.

# Whose Nostalgia Is It, Anyway?

Original Post Date Aug. 27, 2011

A side bar in this week's *Advertising Age* made me sit up and take notice. The main article was on the Pan Am brand and new TV programs scheduled for this fall that are tapping into a nostalgia trend. On its face, this is nothing to write home about. Or more to the point, nothing to blog about. What caught my eye in the side bar was the elaboration about nostalgia.

Before I plunge into that, let me provide some context. Influenced in part by the success of the AMC TV series *Mad Men* about the advertising business in the sixties, at least two new shows on major networks this fall hark back to that same era. One is *Pan AM* (ABC). The other is *The Playboy Club* (NBC).

I've seen the promos for these shows. They remind me that I wanted to be an airline stewardess—that's what they were called back then—because I longed to travel the world, but I wasn't tall enough. Even as the height requirements dropped yearly as airline travel exploded, they never got close to 5' 2" in stocking feet. And yes, we always wore stockings. Pantyhose had not yet been invented. Even in heels I would barely have stood higher than the beverage cart. *"Has anyone seen the stew?"* would have echoed up and down the aisle. And yes, there was only one aisle back then.

One of the first Playboy Clubs was about a half hour from my home, but I never had a desire to be a bunny. Despite what you're thinking and although true, that was not because I failed to meet the minimum physiological requirements for that profession, too. Likewise it was not because they didn't make bunny tails sufficiently poufy to cover my ample posterior. We could have clumped three of them together, after all.

Enough about my anatomy. Let's talk nostalgia. The *Ad Age* sidebar by Brian Steinberg opined: *"...nostalgia is a powerful lure to reach the 40-something... upper end of the advertiser-coveted 18-to-49 audience..."* Bad enough he's rubbing it in our faces that after age 50, we're not considered valuable targets anymore, but it gets worse.

Steinberg quoted Denis Riney, a brand consultant, with a point worth bringing to the forefront in this nostalgia discussion. *"Brands like Pan Am and Playboy are emotional signposts that transport us back to an era when America was No. 1."* Riney went on to reference *"the swagger of the Rat Pack era"* and what was then considered a classy lifestyle.

Hang on. Steinberg just said that the networks are using nostalgia to lure 40-somethings, but those "nostalgia" shows are about the sixties and seventies. The sixties are when the Sinatra Rat Pack was swaggering, too. The oldest 40-somethings were still having bed-wetting accidents in the sixties and the youngest were just popping out of their mothers' ovens in the early seventies.

The same advertisers that cast us aside like a pair of old saddle shoes are now co-opting our nostalgia. They can't seriously believe that shows about those decades are going to provide "emotional signposts" for these kids. Apparently they do.

Google "emotional signpost" and you'll find pages about the stages of labor—as in popping out babies—and links to YouTube videos for a song of that title by a techie musician who goes by Gannon. These sites are far more likely to be of interest to 40-somethings than Pan Am stewardesses or Playboy bunnies. Hello, advertisers, are you listening?

Enough, I say! I have absolutely no desire to watch either *Pan Am* or *The Playboy Club**. But if those of us over 50, and especially those over 60 and 70, watch these shows in large enough numbers, we can mess up the audience delivery metrics big time.

The networks will likely guarantee their advertisers some nostalgic percentage of viewers in that coveted 40-something audience. The actual figures, skewed by all of us, dear readers—or rather, viewers—will be vastly depressed for the coveted group, and wonderfully inflated for the age group that truly owns this nostalgia. The advertisers may actually schedule some ads that are targeted to us, if they can figure out what those should be.

Here are some hints. Where did Pan Am fly in the sixties and seventies and what travel bargains can get us there today? If you put Giada De Laurentiis in a bunny costume in my kitchen, what fabulous dish would she be cooking and where can we find the ingredients? What kind of wine should we be drinking with that meal and out of what shape glass?

If advertisers still don't pay attention to us, we should speak out with one voice and tell them where they can stick their emotional signposts. I'll drink to that.

*\* Ed's note: Turns out, no one wanted to watch the bunnies. The show was canclled by week three.*

# Epilogue

## Just One Tasteful Tattoo

People over fifty should not be required to have pictures taken for identification purposes. I know what you're thinking. *"Everyone feels her ID picture is awful."* Mine always are awful, and the older I get, the worse they are. My husband, who loved me even when I was bald from chemotherapy, actually once suggested that I "lose" my driver's license and pay for a new photo. I'd prefer to have a microchip implanted and take my chances with Big Brother.

Maybe I watch too much TV, but shows like CSI have story lines built around identifying bodies that turn up without any photo IDs. In the really gory episodes, there's not even a face for anyone to recognize. It made me wonder, if my body turned up that way, how would I be identified? I could see the reports, one more post-mortifying than the next.

If I disappeared, investigators would note: *"The only photo of the missing woman is a college health class picture, labeled 'Severe Backward-C-Curve Posture,' also known as sway back."* Or maybe: *"Police are seeking the whereabouts of senior-aged female with left earlobe pierced 1/8" lower than the right and on a slight angle away from the face."*

The write-up of my demise would read: *"The decomposing body was identified by the victim's sister, who recognized the U-shaped scar on the right foot, made by a broken milk bottle when the victim, then aged twelve and already showing signs of extreme clumsiness, failed to execute a full pirouette around the back porch post."*

Worse yet, I envisioned: *"The decapitated body was positively identified through the intricate network of stretch marks on the upper abdomen and lateral thigh areas, which conformed precisely to the indentations on a pair of control-top pantyhose found in the laundry basket of a local woman missing since last month."*

Perhaps it would read: *"Dental records proved conclusively that the four root canals and six full crowns in the body dredged from the canal matched the mouth of a female executive who disappeared shortly after a sales presentation."*

Or: *"Former co-workers agreed that the aromatic blend of nervous perspiration, Right Guard, Obsession and Listerine could have emanated from only one body. A retired police dog confirmed the match."*

Sadly for many, life is too ephemeral to assume you'll go to your grave as the result of old age. Violence, mayhem, carnage surround us daily. Anyone could become a crime or accident statistic at any time. A premature exit from this life would be bad enough. The prospect of such ignominious identification would have me rolling over in my proverbial grave. I needed to find a better way to identify my body.

I considered coloring my hair fuchsia, and rejected it. On a young person, that would be exotic. On someone my age, it would be looked upon as eccentric, at best. Rhinestones embedded in my pinky fingernails seemed viable. Fashionable women of all ages are doing odd things to their nails today. By week two, the manicure had deteriorated to the look of recycled Mylar.

Next came the plan to cultivate a "trademark" of exotic lingerie. The implementation stage fell short; or more correctly, the leopard print bikinis did. And the imitation French lace bras (all my budget could handle) scratched so badly I developed a hideous rash—hardly an image to punch out on. What really killed the plan, however, was the realization that no one would know me in exotic lingerie anyway. I envisioned family and close friends agreeing: *"That couldn't be her. She always wore Bridget Jones briefs and cotton bras..."*

Then I remembered a news story from decades ago. A young WAC had been murdered, her body found under a blanket in a car abandoned at a major airport. She was identified through a tattoo of a black panther with blood dripping from its claws. It had seemed an oddly romantic touch to an otherwise seamy story. I couldn't help wondering why a woman would get such a tattoo. I had fantasized about the exotic life she must have led, especially since it drove her husband to murder her, as it turned out.

Just one discreetly located and tastefully rendered tattoo should do it, I decided, if the subject was suitably obscure. After all, tattoos are common now, though not for my generation, and they're usually stamped somewhere I wouldn't consider.

The forensic specialists studying my remains would report: *"The victim was identified through a tattoo of a lorikeet, a rare tropical bird of exotic plumage..."* and everyone would fantasize about the exciting life I must have led. Of course, with my luck, some hotshot reporter would insist it was a red-footed booby.

# Acknowledgments

Thank you to all my readers who provided feedback on *RetirementSparks* posts during its inaugural year.

Special thanks to Joe Petteruti and to the late H. Peter Olsen for reading almost all of these and for letting me know you did. You encouraged me to keep on posting. That discipline is what led to this book.

Thanks also to Joe and to Becky Eckstein, Lynne Fraser, Fred Friedman and my husband, Jagdish Sachdev, for providing those extra sets of eyes to edit this book. You went the extra mile to help me reach the finish line on schedule. I raise my glass to you!

# Notes

# Notes

# About the Author

After graduating from Brown University, Elaine M. Decker lived and worked in the metro NY area for 25 years. A New Jersey native, Ms. Decker relocated to Providence, RI in 1992, where she lives with her husband and cats. She recently retired from nonprofit management. This followed earlier careers in computer programming and systems, and marketing and communications. Retirement heralds her fourth career—as a freelance writer. She's been writing social satire for decades. Her work has appeared in such publications as *The New York Times*, *Marketing News* and *The Privacy Journal.* Selections from her blog RetirementSparks.blogspot.com appear in the monthly RI publication, *Prime Time.*

Made in the USA
Charleston, SC
18 January 2012